Gucci

BY GUCCI

BY GUCCI

85 years of Gucci

Creative Direction by Douglas Lloyd

Texts by Sarah Mower

Editorial Coordination by Gucci

In honour of the publication of this book, Gucci is pleased to make a significant donation to
The Film Foundation for the restoration of "A Woman under the Influence" directed by John Cassavetes, 1974

Thames & Hudson

TABLE OF CONTENTS

QUALITY IS REMEMBERED LONG
AFTER PRICE IS FORGOTTEN

ALDO GUCCI

UNSEEN GUCCI

Beneath the drama that has accompanied the rise of Gucci to international fame lies another dimension of image and memory that has never been explored. These untold narratives, stretching back 85 years to 1921, are contained in Gucci's private archive, a collection that, since 1997, has been meticulously reassembled, documented and preserved as a company DNA-bank in a quiet suburb of Milan.

Step through the door, and the first sight, standing on its own pedestal and framed under Plexiglas, is a single, immaculate white pigskin bamboo-handled bag. This breathtaking edition of the bag that became a Gucci house signature is dated 1947. Inspired by the shape of a saddle and codenamed 0633, it is, with its matching bamboo turn-key lock and curvilinear functionality, a landmark design that took Gucci to international recognition in the hands of social sophisticates and movie stars – on and off the screen. Ingrid Bergman carried a Gucci bamboo-handled bag in Roberto Rossellini's *Voyage to Italy* in 1953; it was part of Vanessa Redgrave's mini-skirted mod look in *Blow Up*–a sharp contemporary detail flashing across Antonioni's brilliantly heightened 1966 mirror-image of swinging London. Nearby stands a trophy with a different significance: the soignée-sporty G1327 "envelope" bag of the kind caressed by a glacial beauty in the pages of *Vogue* in 1961 – a design with two discreetly identifiable strips of green-red-green equestrian webbing that helped win Gucci a coveted place on the mid-century uptown American list of desirables. Further along again stands a major Gucci proto-star, the shoulderbag codenamed G1244, also in 1961. This casually chic beige canvas bag, with its rounded corners, brown pigskin trim and a tubular springcatch, was an idea originally drawn, like so much else of Gucci's stock, from the stable-yard – in this case, a horse's nosebag. Easy to dip into and to tuck neatly under the arm, the G1244 arrived with perfect timing, ideally honed to fit women's accelerating lives and increasingly young way of dressing in a way no ladies' bag had done before. This is the design, of course, that became a favourite of Jackie Onassis throughout the Sixties and Seventies – a bag so adored and accumulated by her that it became integral to her vastly influential style. When it was relaunched and named the "Jackie O" in her honour in 1996, it hit new highs of frantic fashionability and continues to be reinvented to this day.

Close up, the power of these few telling objects lies in their ability to telescope time. Both exemplars of the Italian craftsmanship and aesthetics of their moment, they are historical landmarks in a way – yet still fresh enough to drive any contemporary vintage-lover to thoughts of smash-and-grab. Bags like these, and the hundreds of pieces of leather goods, luggage, accessories and clothes contained in this treasure-house of fashion still carry the *frisson* of excitement that has lured a continuous stream of fashionable people through Gucci's doors from its beginnings and into the 21st century. Many ingeniously deploy Gucci's house symbols: bamboo, the green-red-green webbing, horsebits and the famous GG initials that were originated by Guccio Gucci from the late Twenties onwards. They were handmade at Gucci work-benches in Florence, constructed in the finest materials – the characteristic brindled pigskin, soft, unmarkable "cuoio grasso" calf, canvas, ostrich and finest reptile skins – but there is something more that burnishes their fascination beyond their intrinsic technical excellence. The reason Gucci become imprinted on the fashion consciousness of the world is embedded somewhere else – a place indivisibly bound into the roles it has played in the lives of the successful and the glamorous through so many eras. This, of course, is precisely the charge that, between 1992 and 2004, Tom Ford seized and renewed in his own image. Exploding upon young consumers as something completely unknown and unexpected, his vision turned Gucci into a globally-understood synonym for S-E-X and celebrity in the Nineties. Now the Ford chapter (allotted to vast wardrobes containing every men's and women's collection from autumn 1995) can be read again as part of the continuous story of how Gucci has expressed its times, leaving its GG-loafered footprint on multiple layers of social history.

Who has worn Gucci and why? That side of the record jumps to life in a different section of the archive that contains movie stills, magazines, books, catalogues and press-cuttings, painstakingly reassembled by Gucci's research team. Looked at alongside the collection of beautiful examples of historically important leather goods, accessories and clothing, they make a multi-dimensional visual documentary of what the name has meant to generations of Gucci-loving customers. They show how Gucci horsebit bags, loafers, luggage and hipster belts have constantly criss-crossed from the private wardrobes of movie stars into movie-wardrobes themselves. They trace how the status-value of Gucci's products has surfed through wildly differing societies and cultures, its indelible symbols acquired as necessary objects by everyone from royals to rock stars, movie stars to moguls, conservative bankers to rap-stars, in Europe and America, Japan and Asia from the Forties right up to the present moment.

The essence of Gucci's magnetism – that specific, racily glamorous aura – can be traced through wave after wave of international stars right back to the pre-dawn of *La Dolce Vita*. Founded in Florence in 1921, Guccio Gucci's small family luggage and leather goods firm survived World War II to become part of the great post-war upsurge of Italian craftsmanship, design creativity, fashion and movie-making. It was a spontaneous collective movement that launched colour, warmth, and a long-lost sense of life-affirming extravagance into a sensually starved world. The sight of the gorgeousness of Sophia Loren, the suaveness of Marcello Mastroianni, the cool of the Vespa, the sleekness of the Ferrari, the sharpness of Italian tailoring and the mere whiff of espresso, caught from abroad, were over-whelmingly alluring. The name of Gucci became yet another attraction luring American tourists to Italy, a force that transformed the country into the sexiest possible holiday destination of the Fifties – a longing both captured and heightened by the 1953 hit movie *Roman Holiday*, in which Audrey Hepburn and Gregory Peck ran around the city, revelling in the new modern Italian style.

Things tended to happen under the Italian sun, of course – and any hint of scandalous romance only made it all the more tantalising. In 1949, Ingrid Bergman, often photographed carrying Gucci bags with her tweed suits, fell notoriously in love with Roberto Rossellini on the set of *Stromboli*. When she became pregnant by him while still married to Petter Lindstrom, Edwin Johnson of Colorado denounced Bergman on the floor of the Senate as "a free-love cultist". How exciting. The couple's supposed Italian debauch, trailed by photographers, became major American news for a fortnight, even relegating President Truman's announcement of the H-bomb to relative obscurity. When Elizabeth Taylor, then 29, and Richard Burton, also illicitly involved while filming *Cleopatra* in Rome in 1962, were caught in the paparazzi flashbulbs on the Via Veneto in the early hours, she was wearing a matching leopard coat and hat, and carrying a glossy crocodile Gucci handbag. "Liz and Burton frolic in Rome; Kiss, Dance", blared the headlines. (Taylor kept up a Gucci habit when more properly married to Burton, and long after; company employees vividly remember fulfilling a custom-made order from her – for a turquoise lizard purse with a gold horsebit – in the Eighties.)

Nino Vendetti, a Roman journalist who wrote a film column "*La Dolce Vita nella Capitale*" in *La Notte di Milano*, remembers, "We called Rome 'Hollywood on the Tiber' in those years. There were so many movies being made, the city was one big set – and at night, the Via Veneto was like a catwalk. It was better than going to the theatre! The stars would work all day and then go out for an *aperitivo* at the Café de Paris, and all the photographers would swarm around them. It was different then: stars wanted to show themselves off. These days, they're much more private." Naturally enough, when Federico Fellini filmed *La Dolce Vita*, his 1960 chronicle of those decadent days and endless nightlife of paparazzi, aristocrats and celebrities, Gucci was fully on the scene. When Anita Ekberg took a break from flaunting her super-voluptuous form in the Trevi fountain, she – like every other Cinecittà goddess at the time – dropped into the store to treat herself to something Gucci. The evidence is caught in an 'off-duty' publicity photograph snapped at night while she perched, laughing, on the bonnet of a sports car, wearing Capri pants and a straining sweater, flirtatiously juggling a toy poodle in one hand – and an oversized white, Gucci shoulder bag implanted with a giant horsebit, in the other.

The fact that Gucci is so evident in these photographs is to the credit of Aldo Gucci, the eldest of three sons of the company's founding father, Guccio Gucci. In 1938, Aldo – then an ambitious 33-year-old with a vast instinct for publicity, marketing and branding well ahead of his time – had the foresight to push his more conservative father to open a store at a premises he'd found at number 21, Via Condotti. ("It's not a secret," Aldo once boasted, "I do possess a determined quality, sensitivity, a creative mind and plenty of good taste.") The Rome store was to be the first outside the family's home town, Florence – the city which has remained the company's manufacturing base since 1921. Though the timing – on the brink of World War II – would have paralysed a more timid entrepreneur, Aldo Gucci had adamantine confidence in the psychological attractions of his family's handcrafted wares. In spite of current conditions, he glimpsed a triumphant future: if people felt convinced by the intrinsic value of a luxury product, they'd buy, no matter what. "Quality is remembered long after price is forgotten," he announced with bravado – a prophetic saying he later had tooled into a leather plaque and proudly displayed in his offices as a constant reminder of just how right he was.

Being in Rome turned out to be a coup. Gucci had secured a prestigious address in the street that was to become the luxury shopping magnet for off-duty actors and actresses making movies at Rome's Cinecittà, the studio-town to the south-east of the capital purpose-built by Mussolini in 1937 to stimulate the national industry. Even before the war, Aldo had looked at Rome and understood its potential. A playground full of aristocrats and cosmopolitan high-spenders, it was a society that, externally at least, revolved around the need to *fare una bella figura* (make a good impression) at the nightly *passeggiata* and evening-long posings at the Café de Paris on the Via Veneto. Added to the elegant one-upmanship at private parties in local *palazzi*, all those occasions for elegant exhibitionism were building demand for hand-made clothes, finely-wrought accessories and fabulous jewels – the latter already catered for by Bulgari, just a few doors along from Gucci's position on the Via Condotti. Wherever those gorgeous women and suave, lady-killing *ragazzi* roamed, day or night – by limousine, convertible or plane – they should be carrying Gucci, Aldo believed. The fact that his youngest brother, Rodolfo, already had an entrée into that world must have honed his thinking further. Sent to Rome on a delivery errand by his father in 1929, Rodolfo had been spotted by a film director and signed up as an actor with the screen-name Maurizio D'Ancora (he appeared in *Rotaie*, a masterpiece of Italian silent cinema, and co-starred with Anna Magnani in *Finalmente Soli* in 1942). By the end of the war, he returned to lend gloss to the family business with a debonair twinkle in his eye and a string of movie-star contacts at the ready.

Still, in 1938, circumstances presented massive tests for Gucci's creativity and lateral thinking. Imported materials had already dried up when the League of Nations imposed sanctions in retaliation to Mussolini's invasion of Abyssinia in 1935, and when the conflagration of World War II reached Italy, matters only worsened. Gucci's Florentine craftsmen, however, were ingeniously resourceful. Directed by Guccio, they used inexpensive, home-grown raffia, wood and specially woven canvas made out of canapa hemp from Naples as substitutes for traditional fine leather and metal components. (This was the era before specially trained leather-goods "designers" existed in the sense we understand now. Instead, the prolific working patterns of Gucci's craftsmen inadvertently speak of the hardship of the times: they are humble pencil sketches recorded in scraped-together hand-stitched notebooks made of rough war-time paper, testament to the age before designs were routinely numbered, registered and patented). Still, even at a point when the country was in post-war economic ruin, someone in the wood-working department made a pivotal breakthrough. An experiment to bend and burnish a piece of bamboo (a commodity then sourceable from Japan) over a Bunsen burner produced the great-looking curved handbag handle that was to become a Gucci trademark forever after.

Photographs of beautiful people popping in and out of Gucci bearing gifts and personal purchases spread its image as a token of wealth and sophisticated living throughout Europe and across America. The potency of those photos is still resonating within Gucci now. When she saw them, Frida Giannini, Gucci's creative director, who took the helm of design in 2005, exclaimed "I recognised the streets, the light, the way women dressed, from my grandmother's albums. Everything was familiar. I was really fascinated." Born in Rome and educated in the city's prestigious Academy of Art, Frida Giannini traces her emotional link to Gucci through the experiences of her mother and grandmothers – as part of the everyday Italian culture of style and fashion. Giannini spends time researching her collections in the archives, sifting through the evocative library of images and examining the makings of the handbags, luggage, jewellery and stores of vintage clothes. "That period, from the Fifties to the Seventies, was unforgettable: the time when celebrities would come to work at Cinecittà, take apartments or villas around Rome and stay for days or months in the city. My grandmother always talked about the Via Veneto, where you could go to bars and cafés in the evening after dinner and always see actors and actresses. It was a very hot period."

Though Gucci is quintessentially Florentine, it was from Rome that its fame radiated worldwide after World War II. Its innovative, elegant accessories were part of the fashion fever that seized the capital, bringing a rush of new *Alta Moda* couture house-openings – Emilio Schuberth (1938), Fontana (1944), Roberto Capucci (1950), Princess Galitzine (1959) and Valentino (1960) among them. Their clients were social thoroughbreds like the swan-necked Marella Agnelli and the curvaceous new Italian stars Sophia Loren, Claudia Cardinale and Monica Vitti, but crucially, it was visiting Americans – men as well as women – who ricocheted the discovery of the new sensual, casual Italian elegance across the world. First in line were de-mobbed American GIs. Deliriously happy and on the loose with dollars to spend, they called at Gucci for its "suiters" – suit-bags, fitted with hangers, in lightweight Gucci canvas smartly identified by the in-house diamond pattern, which proved ideal for carrying their uniforms – as well as to snap up glossy wallets and purses as souvenirs for their wives and sweethearts back home. Then, as American movie-makers began to use Cinecittà, Roman streets and nightclubs were lit up by a constantly changing cast of the world's most beautiful sex symbols: Ava Gardner, Elizabeth Taylor, Grace

Kelly, Ursula Andress and all their attendant co-stars, husbands and lovers. Just as many of the Roman couturiers worked on fitting these modern goddesses for film costumes as well as their "real" life, so Gucci's bags, shoes, luggage and accessories also had a life both on and off camera. From then on, it has racked up dozens of movie appearances that span everything from Italian *Neorealismo* such as Rossellini's *Europa '51* (1952; Ingrid Bergman) and Antonioni's *L'Avventura* (1960; Monica Vitti); to *The VIPs* (1963; Liz Taylor), *What's New Pussycat?* (1965; Romy Schneider), all the way up to *Drugstore Cowboy* (1989 Matt; Dillon) and *Pulp Fiction* (1994; Harvey Keitel).

By the late Sixties, the Rome store was mobbed, struggling to serve 1,800 overexcited customers daily, mostly Americans. *The International Herald Tribune*, announcing the launch of Gucci loafers for women in 1968, urged its readers it was financially worth it to fly to Rome just to grab them. Judith Harris, assigned to describe the Rome phenomenon in *The New York Times* in 1974, detailed a long list of starry regulars. "Princess Grace and her daughter Caroline recently stopped by to stock up on leather handbags and silk shirts, Jackie O and her sister Lee Radziwill are customers, and so is the cinema aristocracy that commutes between Hollywood and Rome's Cinecittà," she reported counting the heads of "Sophia Loren, Jack Lemmon, Henry Fonda, Burt Lancaster (luggage and loafers), Elizabeth Taylor (gifts for friends), Rod Steiger, and Audrey Hepburn, who is married to a Rome psychiatrist and lives here," among the besiegers. Many of the sell-out pieces they were seeking were already well-known classics. A duffel bag – ideal carry-on luggage – had been in production since the Twenties. The phenomenally popular Gucci loafer with its striped webbing and horsebit detail, dated from 1953, and "the feed-bag Jackie O wears", she reported, "has been around for 20 years."

In the meantime, Gucci was stretching its fame and design portfolio in other ways. Rodolfo Gucci lavished his charm and passion for product at the Milan store on the Via Montenapoleone, which opened in 1951. There, he went to the furthest lengths to commission luxurious items to satisfy customers like Gianni Agnelli and Giovanni Agusta (the owner of Agusta helicopters) and the royal Grimaldis. He sourced unique baby-soft crocodile skins in emerald, cherry, green and yellow for a chain-handled bag that had become a glossy Gucci favourite (chain patented number 112362 in 1965; bag codename 0535) of Audrey Hepburn, Liz Taylor, Ursula Andress and Jackie Kennedy (who selected it to carry during some of her official appearances as First Lady). He sold gold jewellery (so refined that a single chain sold for 80 million lire in 1970); had blankets made in wolf or sable and lined in cashmere and vicugna, and ordered kid slippers from the man who made the Pope's – nothing but the best for his customers' feet.

Franco Gittardi (who managed the Milan store before moving with the company to America and Japan) relates how one of Gucci's star products was designed, virtually on the spot, one day in 1966. "Grace of Monaco visited – with Rainier – asking to see Rodolfo's wife Alessandra, who she knew as an actress in their film days. The Princess bought a green pigskin "bamboo" bag – but Rodolfo also pressed her to take a gift. When she relented and asked for a scarf, he was mortified: he didn't think Gucci had anything special enough. The second she left, he got on the phone to Vittorio Accornero – who was a famous children's illustrator he had met when Accornero was working as a movie-set designer – and begged him to get around there with a design for the most beautiful flowered scarf he could create. Next day, Accornero was there, with his painting." It was the "Flora". Accornero's multicoloured flowered template – a huge seller as a silk headscarf alone – was destined for an unimaginably extended future. That began when Gittardi was detailed by Rodolfo to think up ways of applying the print to Gucci products, "I was Mr Flora! We used it on ties, umbrellas, in the form of jewellery, Limoges ashtrays, organza wedding dresses – everything!" Flora kindled such long-lasting affection among European women that they passed it onto their daughters. One was Caroline of Monaco, who wore a blouse in her "mother's" scarf-print as a teenager; another, the much younger Frida Giannini, whose own mother loved the print as a girl in Rome. Re-connecting with that feeling, Giannini revived Flora on printed canvas bags for summer 2005, for which Gucci was met with overwhelming demand. Other Flora variations, re-scaled, re-coloured and abstracted, made it onto Forties/Seventies print dresses for summer 2006, into jewellery and 3-D decorations for evening bags. They were all hits: living proof of the power of a Gucci phenomenon 40 years after it was first dreamed up.

None of that, however, touched the significance of Gucci's take-off in the slipstream of the Jet Set. Throughout the Sixties and Seventies, scarcely an airport photo appeared without GG-printed Gucci luggage among the flurries of fur coats and dark glasses. Gucci flew with Ringo Starr and Maureen Cox with Michael and Shakira Caine. It was carry-on for Sammy Davis Junior, Liza Minnelli

and David Niven. Few, however, were more committed to Gucci-style travelling – or have better memories of that glamorous and vivid moment – than Britt Ekland, the quintessential sexy long-legged blonde mini-skirted Swedish "discovery" who arrived in Rome, aged 24, with her new husband, Peter Sellers. "My love affair with Gucci began because Peter knew it. He had Gucci briefcases, hobo bags, luggage and bags to keep his camera equipment, tape recorders and gadgets in," she recalls. "He was the ultimate consumer! I remember for the first Christmas we were married, in 1964, I gave him a Gucci black crocodile agenda. It cost £80. I thought it was the most money, but I'd worked that year so I bought it."

Ekland and Sellers – chased everywhere by paparazzi – were often photographed shopping in Gucci. "I don't think people now realise that all the celebrity-photographer business we have today actually started in Rome. Italy had celebrity magazines like *Oggi* that needed to be filled every week. I learned very early that if you stopped and let them snap you, they'd be happy and then go away," she says. "And if the photographers were nice, they'd sometimes be let inside the shops." Several evocative archive photographs show her sitting on Gucci's banquettes or crouching by shelves – all tousled mane and mini skirt – to inspect the merchandise. The significance of shopping Gucci was very specific, she remembers. "It was a question of quality and respectability. Gucci was expensive without being showy. It was the only thing I liked. When you looked inside the bags, all the stitching, the linings, all the parts that did not show were beautifully done. And they last! I am still using things I bought then. I had a wonderful black crocodile chain-handled bag I now use as a clutch. A wallet. Wardrobe bags!"

More than anything, Ekland recalls the glamour associated with flying in those days. "You dressed up to travel. You smoked on the plane. I had three Yorkshire terriers that came with me in the cabin. I'd be fully made-up, with two sets of false eyelashes, all the way from London to New York. The whole thing was like a huge party. I'd always have my gorgeous brown leather beauty case, with the green and red stripes, with me. It always made a great foot-rest!" In 1974, Ekland became a Bond Girl. In *The Man with the Golden Gun*, playing the secret agent Mary Goodnight opposite Roger Moore, she found herself working with a movie-wardrobe that included a GG canvas shoulder bag, a horsebit belt and Gucci loafers. "It showed her type: a smart, professional woman," she reflects. (That shoulderbag had an after-life when it was revived, slightly altered, in spring/summer 2000, as part of a capsule collection of monogram accessories calculated to chime with the "logomania" craze that blew up with the economic boom on the cusp of the millennium.) After divorcing Sellers, off-screen, she fully maintained the Gucci habit when flying the world on the arm of her new lover, Rod Stewart. An archive shot of that Glam Rock period shows them arriving at Heathrow airport in 1975, just after Stewart released his smash-hit album, *Atlantic Crossing*. Ekland is wearing a leopard-spot pant-suit she'd had made – and the pair of them are festooned with Gucci bags. Frida Giannini rediscovered that shot when planning her winter 2006/07 Glam-Rock-influenced collection. "Britt Ekland is one of the most iconic beauties in our archive," she declares. One of the bags in the collection is even named "The Britt" in her honour: a shoulder bag with a big, shiny interlocking metal GG that, says Giannini, "represents the disco dance-floor to me."

Would Guccio Gucci have been dismayed by the idea of his baggage, emblazoned with his personal initials, in the hands so many of these glamorous globetrotters? Hardly. Gucci senior had died in 1953, but this scene was the ambition of his poor Italian teenage years, realised on an epic scale. Guccio Gucci first gazed on the travelling-style of the international ultra-wealthy – and the comings and goings of the scandalous celebrities of the late Victorian theatre – while working at the Savoy hotel in London, which had recently opened in the late 1890s. (Lillie Langtry, the bejewelled actress, international pin-up, and famous mistress of the Prince of Wales, kept a suite at the Savoy for "entertaining".) Exactly what job this penniless Tuscan boy (who had left home in Florence after his father's straw hat-making business went bankrupt) did there has been variously described as dishwasher, waiter, bellboy or maitre d'. There are no records to confirm it. Still, the salient idea Guccio Gucci took back from London to Italy is in no doubt. It was there, stacked high, daily, in the hotel lobby: the luxurious handmade bespoke leather initial-embossed and crested trunks, suitcases, hatboxes, vanity cases and all manner of specialised travelling equipment that accompanied the theatre aristocracy, lords and ladies of the British Empire, crowned heads of Europe and India, and the new super-rich entrepreneurs and industrialists of America on their leisurely progress around the world by ocean liner, trans-continental locomotive and the new-fangled motor car.

He could do that, Guccio thought. Hailing – proudly – from a part of Tuscany that had had leather craftsmanship at its fingertips for centuries, he eventually returned to Florence to work at a leather-craft company, becoming expert in choosing hide and grading leather, and gaining experience as the shop's branch manager in Rome. By 1921, he had scraped enough finance together to inaugurate his own shop in Via Vigna Nuova in Florence. The opening was proudly announced in an advertisement that declared Guccio's ambition to be part of the world of the upper-class Anglocentric tastes – the luxury fashion of the time. In impeccably elegant art deco lettering, it announced: GUCCIO GUCCI VALIGERIA INGLESE.

Crucially for the future identity of the business, not long after, Gucci also perceived the status attached to the sporting pursuits of his leisured customers. Observing their particular obsession with equestrian pursuits, by the late Twenties he was incorporating the imagery of saddlery and riding tack into his products. These were the references that were fast to define the style of the house – the saddle-leather, the stitching, the brass horsebits and stirrups, the shapes of saddle-bags and nosebags, and, as a stroke of genius, the canvas webbing of girth-straps, chosen in green-red-green stripes – identifiable at 20 yards with a single glance. Gucci's window displays played this up, deploying harnesses, hunting horns and guns as props. In fact, the Guccis liked hunting, particularly Guccio's son Vasco (who was placed in the family between Aldo and Rodolfo), who spent much time with his guns and dogs in the hills around Tuscany, and later acquired a hunting lodge outside Florence. This was the material around which the irrepressible Aldo later would weave the towering myth that the family, back in the mists of mediaeval times, became saddle-makers to renaissance princes – the story he spun within the hearing of journalists at every possible opportunity when he took Gucci to conquer America. (An early Gucci faux "family crest" used in the Fifties made passing, perhaps humorous reference to the legend: a knight in armour, carrying an attaché case in one hand and a duffel bag in the other. Its image dangled on zipper tags right up to the Eighties.)

After conquering Rome, Aldo arrived, buoyed up on confidence and family pride, as a pioneer of Italian luxury brands in America, ready to open a Gucci store at 7, East 58th Street in New York, in 1953. Advertisements in *Vogue* were immediately reciprocated with editorial fashion pages, giving Gucci an unconditional passport into the seamlessly correct circles of upscale society. A happy addition to the town-and-country dress code, the famous bamboo-handled bag was ushered into the editorial pages of May 1954, "to wear with a crisp, quiet, button-through linen sheath". Fashion cognoscenti were early adopters: Edith Head (who kept her personal sketches for costume designs safe in a Gucci briefcase while trotting to and from Paramount), put Fred Astaire in a pair of soft-soled Gucci moccasins to dance opposite Audrey Hepburn in *Funny Face* in 1957. Gucci's place in the WASP-y fashion universe was settled in August 1958, when *Vogue* asked, "Who are the dashing women of the USA?" and answered itself with a photostory on "Mrs A Willard Mellor, ex-model and weathervane for *Vogue*'s country clothes report", an ideal housewife of irreproachable taste, who ran errands in tweeds, kilts and cardigans, briskly whisking a Gucci handbag in her wake.

Mission accomplished – with soaring sales – among the sophisticates of New York, Aldo Gucci moved on to Florida in 1961, to capture another exclusive clientele: the inhabitants of Palm Beach. Gene Pressman, whose family owned the menswear store Barneys (which developed into the sine qua non of hip designer specialty stores in Nineties New York) witnessed the scene as a child in the mid-Sixties: "The Gucci loafer with the green-red-green band with the metal bit was the ultimate shoe for the Palm Beach elitist. It was a status thing, the Rolls-Royce of fashion. Italians always made the best leather goods. I remember it being simultaneous with Pucci, with images of the French Riviera. All the playboys wore Gucci loafers." One of these was the flamboyant Aldo himself, who settled in to live the life in Palm Beach between business trips. *The Miami Herald* scanned him top-to-toe in a profile dated April 20th, 1974. "His shoes," it reported , "are a badge bespeaking extravagance, a touch of insouciance, and the sure knowledge: 'we are here to play'."

The extent to which Gucci registered among American men added to its well-placed niche as accessory to women's fashion, giving it an enviable double-edge almost no competitor could rival. The loafer became a much-discussed social marker. Richard A Shortway, *Vogue*'s publisher and owner of six pairs, gave a pithy insight into its powers of communication at the kind of executive meetings he'd attend. "It's an easy read – not like flashing your Tank watch, which you have to raise your cuffs to do," he told *The New York Times* in June 1978. As in all matters of menswear though, a guy had to be careful of context, and even geography. John T Molloy, a counsellor on "problems of dress" who advised companies such as General Motors, AT&T and Merrill Lynch, and made his name out of his 1975 handbook, *Dress for Success*, cautioned: "In the most ultra-sophisticated cities, shoes with tassels, or shoes with Mr Gucci's rather chic initials are perhaps – just possibly- acceptable for some men. Elsewhere," he intoned, "they should be studiously avoided."

So successful were those $89 loafers – both for men, and for women who wanted a comfortable, low-heeled shoe – that Gucci found it necessary to hive off the footwear department into its own store in New York in 1968. The following year 84,000 pairs were sold across America; 24,000 in New York alone. The men's-for-women style attracted understated dressers, such as Lauren Bacall (who bought several pairs she later donated to the Museum at the Fashion Institute of Technology), while conformist New York schoolgirls embraced it as uniform. "It was a social landmark for Chapin girls. It showed your status level – that preppy bit loafer," remembers the *Vogue* fashion editor, Tonne Goodman, a teenager at the time. When 18-year-old Martina Navratilova announced her defection from Czechoslovakia in 1975, press reports logged the Gucci bag slung on her shoulder and Gucci loafers on her feet as unmissable signals of her entry to the USA – and the money. Even as the economy plunged deep into the recession caused by the oil crisis, its followers never flinched. "At Gucci, You'd Think People Had Money to Burn", boggled *The New York Times* in the winter of 1974. Even the notoriously supercilious attitude of the retail staff (Gucci was dubbed "The Rudest Store in New York" by Mimi Sheraton in the *New York*), couldn't deter them. "It's masochism", snapped a young New York "career woman" canvassed by the paper. "If you want to pay by cheque, they ask for your blood type." She was, however, still in the queue. By this time, Gucci was a fully-fledged American craze that had spread far beyond the tweedy town-and-country set. It was turning louche, sexy, a touch dangerous at the edges. In 1968, it had opened on Rodeo Drive in swanky style, a momentous step that propelled Gucci into clothing for the first time in its history. Back in Florence, the youngest of Aldo's three sons, Paolo, restless to expand into ready-to-wear, began adding pieces, like GG printed shirts, patchwork A-line suede and leather skirts, snake and fur-trimmed coats and skirts to Gucci's range. Paolo hired Alberta Ballerini, whose mother had worked for Princess Galitzine in Rome, to assist. "It was really only items, not really a collection," she remembers. "Paolo and I would fight over taste. He loved all these metal accessories and GGs on the clothes, and enamel buttons, and I'd try to take them off." It was the entrance of the total GG top-to-toe look – taking in everything from diamond-and-monogram-printed hats to suits to boots, to matching golf caddies, should you so wish. In Florence, craftsman Roberto Lunghi revealed to a reporter the existence of "A young lady whose sole task is to think up new ways to adorn the Gucci goods with the GG initials and the Gucci colours."

In March 1973, Gucci held a fashion presentation at the St Regis hotel. The indefatigable Eugenia Sheppard of the *New York Post* was astonished. "Up to now," she wrote, "Gucci has been the absolute citadel of the solid little low-heeled brogue with the metal touch that is borrowed from the stable...the classics are still the thing, but they're really going female...all the slacks have a new cut Gucci calls bikini." There was a slinky white kid safari suit, and even things for "Gucci man" – a fellow with a Zapata moustache, heavy sideburns and a full chest of hair – who was photographed "relaxing in a fine cotton tiger-pattern sport suit. His calf shoes have side metal trim and he wears a giant marina chain around his neck." Still, among some of the items that now look amusing, there always were Gucci's outstandingly exceptional leather coats, which, in good condition, command upwardly-spiralling prices to this day. Some of the best, Franco Gittardi remembers, were made in ostrich, cobra or baby crocodile. "They were belted, with a sterling silver and enamel snake-head buckle and closure at the neck – with matching shoes. I remember selling them for $1,000 in 1971 – but that was just for the suede ones." Other variations took in-house techniques to wonderful extremes – like treating moss-green suede to an all-over burnout pattern of GGs, and finishing the looks with toggles and buckles in the shape of tigers and leopards. (Those long-forgotten metallic animal motifs, rediscovered and re-appreciated after 20 years when the archive was being assembled, reared their heads to roaring accolades, when they were reincorporated into the elaborate horsebit bags of spring/summer 2004).

In 1977, Aldo amped up the wattage of the Beverly Hills store, installing a glass-walled "Gucci Gallery" above the main floor, to which only privileged customers gained entry with a gold key. Stepping out of the private lift, they were confronted by a $15,000 platinum fox fur draped over the railing, Modigliani, de Chirico and de Kooning hanging on the beige suede walls, and were able to browse through such items as an $11,000 dollar bag on a detachable gold and diamond chain which could double as a choker. Rita Hayworth, John Wayne, Julie Andrews and Michael Caine were among those reported to have taken the opportunity.

By the late Seventies, times were shifting. As Jackie Onassis was being snapped going about her business by Ron Galella, Gucci bag tucked under her arm in Manhattan, across town, the disco boom was taking off at Studio 54. Glenn O'Brien described the fevered goings-on for *Rolling Stone*, "It was a universe of infinite possibilities, where you might meet anyone, where you might do things you hadn't imagined...Margaret Trudeau with no underwear on. Michael Jackson lurking in the DJ booth. People having sex on the balcony. Bianca Jagger riding a horse across the dancefloor." Only incredible dressers and dancers got past the red ropes, of course. Nile Rodgers – himself there, night after night – nailed the scene in a perfect aural snapshot, "He's the Greatest Dancer", the disco anthem he wrote and produced with Bernie Edwards for Sister Sledge in 1979. The sister cooed and panted over the moves and magnetic style of a dressed-to-kill disco stud, working up to the glorious chant about his favoured designer labels: Halston, Gucci, Fiorucci.

Gucci was crossing into black culture for the first time. While other slices of society – the conservative ladies and the rising class of feminist executives - cut sensibly around town with their comfortable Gucci shoes and executive briefcases, young, black aspirational New Yorkers saw the super-fly, logo-loaded, over-the-top glamour of Gucci, and made it their own. In that bizarre transitional time, the hippest and the most establishment types both obliviously agreed with one another on Gucci's absolute suitability to their own wildly divergent lifestyles. For the bodacious, there were white triangle bikinis, strung together with gold GG chains. There was the outrageous $22,900 limited-edition Gucci Cadillac Seville, fitted with "24-carat gold-plated GG wheel covers, horsebits on the fenders, green-red-green stripes and a Gucci signature on the dashboard": it proved the ideal purchase for Sammy Davis Junior. Meanwhile, Nancy Reagan loved her Gucci, too. In December 1980, when Ronald was elected President for the first time, she made an emergency dash to Gucci in Rodeo Drive. The store was closed for two hours while the about-to-be First Lady picked out a size six herringbone topcoat accented with plush leather, a silk afternoon dress in fuchsia and gold, featuring a flower petal neckline, a gold belt and matching shoes, and to go with her white gown for the Inaugural Ball, a white GG bag.

But Jet-Set Gucci was about to hit heavy turbulence. By the early Eighties, knock-offs were everywhere, warfare had broken out within the family, and Aldo Gucci took the disastrous decision to launch a line of cheaper products that flooded the US market. In Europe, however, the name maintained its cachet – but only if you belonged to a certain class. In Britain, Peter York and Ann Barr, of *Harpers & Queen* magazine hilariously dissected the importance of Gucci in *The Official Sloane Ranger Handbook* of 1982, which included helpful explanatory still-lives of GG buckle belts, Jackie O bags, silk scarves and loafers from the Old Bond Street store. Examining their stereotypical Sloanes, "Caroline" and "Henry", in forensic sociological detail, they wrote, "How can one really understand a person wearing the wrong shoes? Others notice ties or lapels; Sloanes notice shoes. Caroline lives in Gucci." The appeal, they concluded, all went back to the upper-crust love of the horse – the relationship Guccio Gucci had understood from the beginning. "The classic Gucci loafer, beloved of Sloanes from the mid-Sixties on and still worn, appealed because it had that smart but military equine look, like a good piece of uniform with regimental brass. And there's literally no limit to the application of horse symbols," they wrote. "You can have snaffles all over your Gucci shirt. You can have it in jacquard, woven all over your luggage. Gucci is fine as long as you anglicise it. You don't want to look like one of those sunstreaked Pignatelli types." A portrait of the über-Sloane goddess, the young Princess of Wales – then a sweet-faced 20-year-old with a penchant for printed Gucci handbags – was on the cover. (Diana's affection for Gucci stayed with her. She was photographed hopping out of a car in Rome carrying a bamboo-handled shopping tote on a visit in 1996.)

In Italy, too, Gucci was strictly the preserve of conservative types. Neil Barrett, a Briton who joined as menswear designer in 1990, saw his brief as "thinking how to dress your father. A 40-to-80-year-old man. A stodgy man. But Gucci was still a status-symbol for Italians." (Although Barrett does remember making an outfit for Michael Jackson: a gold leather biker jacket, gold loafers and white and gold logo jeans at the same time.) Underground, though, both in London and New York, the name of Gucci had acquired currency among very different groups. Kim Hastreiter, editor of the style-bible, *Paper*, recalls in her retrospective, "*20 Years of Style: the world according to Paper*", that in 1984, "the kids in Harlem and the Bronx who were birthing the hip-hop scene had little money to buy luxury labels, so they invented a smart and rad new style that turned status upside down in the face of white establishment. They began to turn up on the street and at rap concerts decked out in bootleg luxury logos... they plastered these all over their casual sports clothes."

A tailor named Dapper Dan became Harlem's most famous converter of labels. The equivalent black British logo-mashers were the B-boys, examples of whose customised fake-Gucci tracksuits have been collected by the V&A costume department. Even though this trend was antithetical to trademark law, as Hastreiter pointed out, it was done in admiration. The benefit of Gucci's high unofficial approval-rating among urban audiences came right back to Gucci 10 or 15 years later. When the hip-hop outsiders become multi-millionaires, they put authentic Gucci at the top of their shopping list.

Back in Florence, in 1993, Maurizio Gucci, son of Rodolfo, and the last of the family members in the business, finally sold his shares to Investcorp. As the *Vogue* editor and fashion historian Hamish Bowles recalls, Gucci was by then "desperately unfashionable", and on the verge of bankruptcy. Yet, in its darkest hour, insider fashion-think was about to circle back and look at Gucci in a new way. The stirrings began in a flare-up of interest in the loafers, but this time, it was generated by the people – fashion assistants, designers and stylists – who were beginning to trawl flea markets for vintage finds. Bowles remembers buying a white pair on his travels. Marcus Von Ackerman, then a menswear editor, recalls, "I started wearing them again – in an ironic way. At that time, they were only for brash City types from Fulham. Nobody else. It was so not cool. But I wore them with jeans and no socks, thinking of Onassis in Capri, with white trousers and no socks. The difference was that you could do it if you weren't 40. You only got it if you knew what went on in the Fifties – it was an insider signal of that." Meanwhile, young women were buying into the Gucci idea, too. Kim Stringer, then an editor on British *Elle*, remembers wearing her loafers as a knowing contradiction, pairing them with her avant-garde black leggings and Yohji Yamamoto oversized shirts.

Across in Los Angeles, the stock of Gucci's retro-fashion credibility was rising, too. The influential vintage dealer Cameron Silver of Decades was in the vanguard of the revival. "In the mid-Nineties a lot of people wanted vintage design; they were interested in all those old codes again. I remember an original GG trenchcoat I sold for $800. It would be worth three times that now. I have a Seventies Gucci ostrich coat I'll never get rid of." This new hunger to collect the beautifully-made clothes and accessories of the past, this treasuring of the kind of design that could stir up emotional associations, was the beginning of a cycle that was to shape the future of fashion. Young designers – like their contemporaries in post-modern art and the music-meisters who were making new sounds out of sampling old – fed new excitement into their collections by quoting, remixing and stirring up fabulous fashion memories in their audience. And no one understood how to do that better than Tom Ford.

Under new management, Gucci was regrouping and reorganising. It hired Dawn Mello, an executive from Bergdorf Goodman, who in turn brought in Tom Ford, a young designer with experience at Cathy Hardwick and Perry Ellis, who worked quietly behind the scenes, starting in Florence in 1992. Gears began to shift perceptibly when, in 1994, Domenico De Sole, a high-flying lawyer who had been CEO of Gucci America Inc moved to Italy as the group's chief operating officer. De Sole and Ford formed a personal understanding that would go on to make corporate history. Once Ford was in control, he turned the collections – and the marketing of Gucci – into a turbo charged, modernised vision of everything he had known and loved about the slick, glamorous Seventies American heyday of a label he had assimilated as a child. Working to re-energise the company codes, Ford began buying back Gucci originals, the kind of pieces he had admired from afar as a kid in Austin, Texas (he had demanded a pair of white Gucci loafers from his parents at the age of 12) and later, as a wide-eyed junior sybarite in New York, in the last days of Studio 54. When he unleashed his first, overwhelming hit of a show of autumn/winter 1995/96 on the fashion press in Milan, Amber Valletta walked out, blonde, blowdried hair bouncing, in a green mohair coat slinkily, unbuttoned satin blouse, midnight velvet bootcut hipsters, and her thumbs hooked in a low-riding belt fastened with a massive silver horsebit. The message was unmistakable. In Ford's own words, it was "cool, movie-star, jet set". Gucci was back.

It's here that the story comes full circle. The first vintage pieces reassembled in the late Nineties formed the beginnings of the Gucci archive, which, as the success of the company grew, has been professionally organised, re-housed and expanded into a comprehensive library of all its multi-faceted pasts. Now, it is the central Gucci DNA-store, an invaluable source of rediscoveries as the design baton passes onto the next generation. In 2006, it is Frida Giannini, a young Italian woman, who holds the keys. When she disappears inside among the bamboo-handled bags and the fox-trimmed coats, what she brings out is yet one more personal re-telling of the story that has always been at the heart of Gucci's legacy.

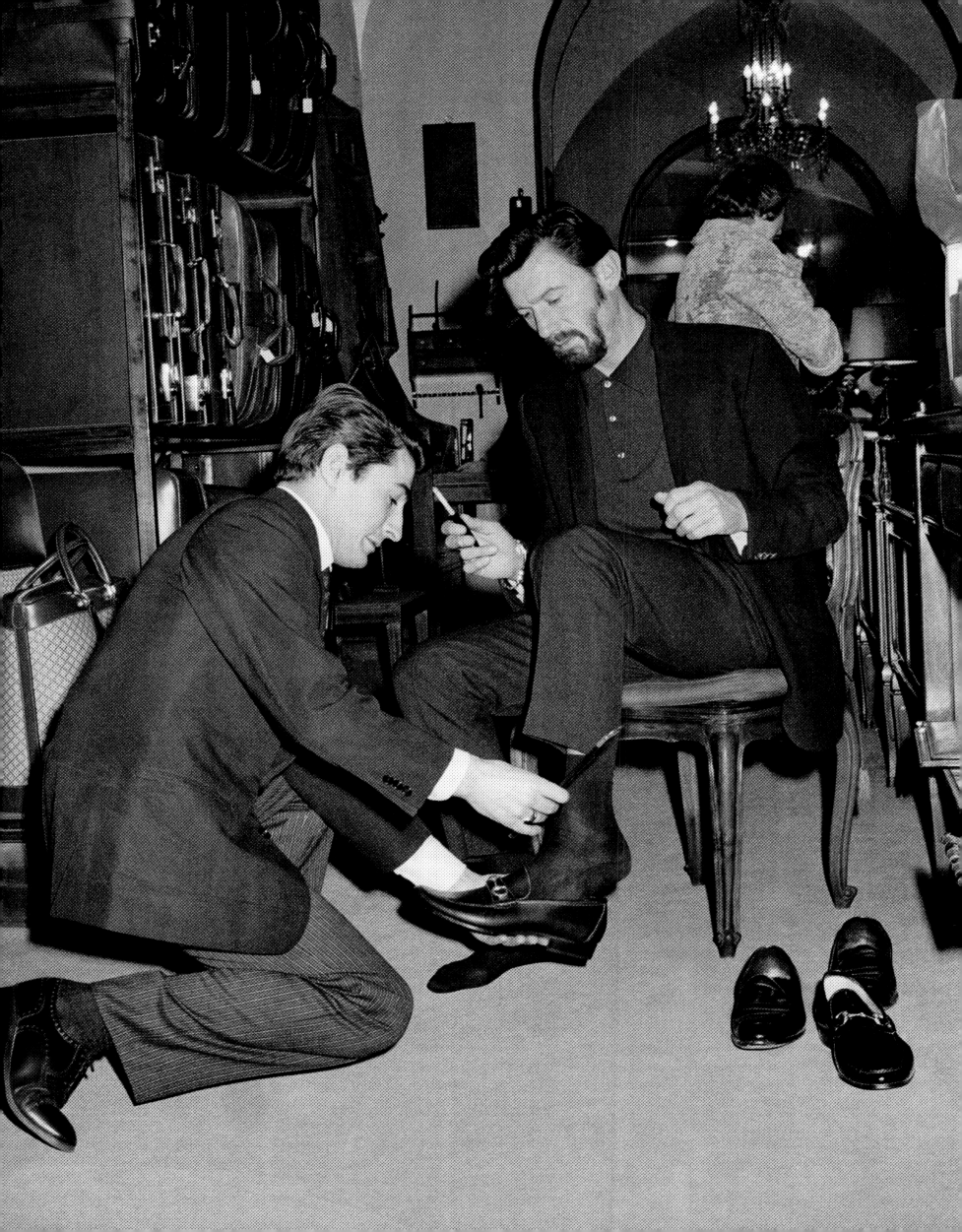

To Mueia Messer
Your leather is
beautiful!
Many thanks
Clark Gable

THE RICH CACHE OF PAPARAZZI,
ADVERTISING AND FASHION
IMAGES ARCHIVED AT GUCCI
CONTAINS HUNDREDS OF
MEMORIES THAT HAVE BECOME
WOVEN INTO ITS IDENTITY. SEEN
TOGETHER, THEY READ AS A
LEXICON OF THE MOVIE-STAR
CONNECTIONS, LANDMARK DESIGN

MOMENTS AND METICULOUS CRAFTSMANSHIP THAT MAKE UP ITS VISUAL LANGUAGE. THE FOLLOWING PAGES DOCUMENT THE INCIDENTS, INSPIRATIONS AND INNOVATIONS THAT HAVE REVERBERATED THROUGH GUCCI DESIGN FROM ITS BEGINNINGS TO THE PRESENT DAY...

VOGUE

PARIS

rs N°845

STAR attitude

Spécial mode & beauté : or, paillettes, strass, soir...
tous les secrets pour briller.

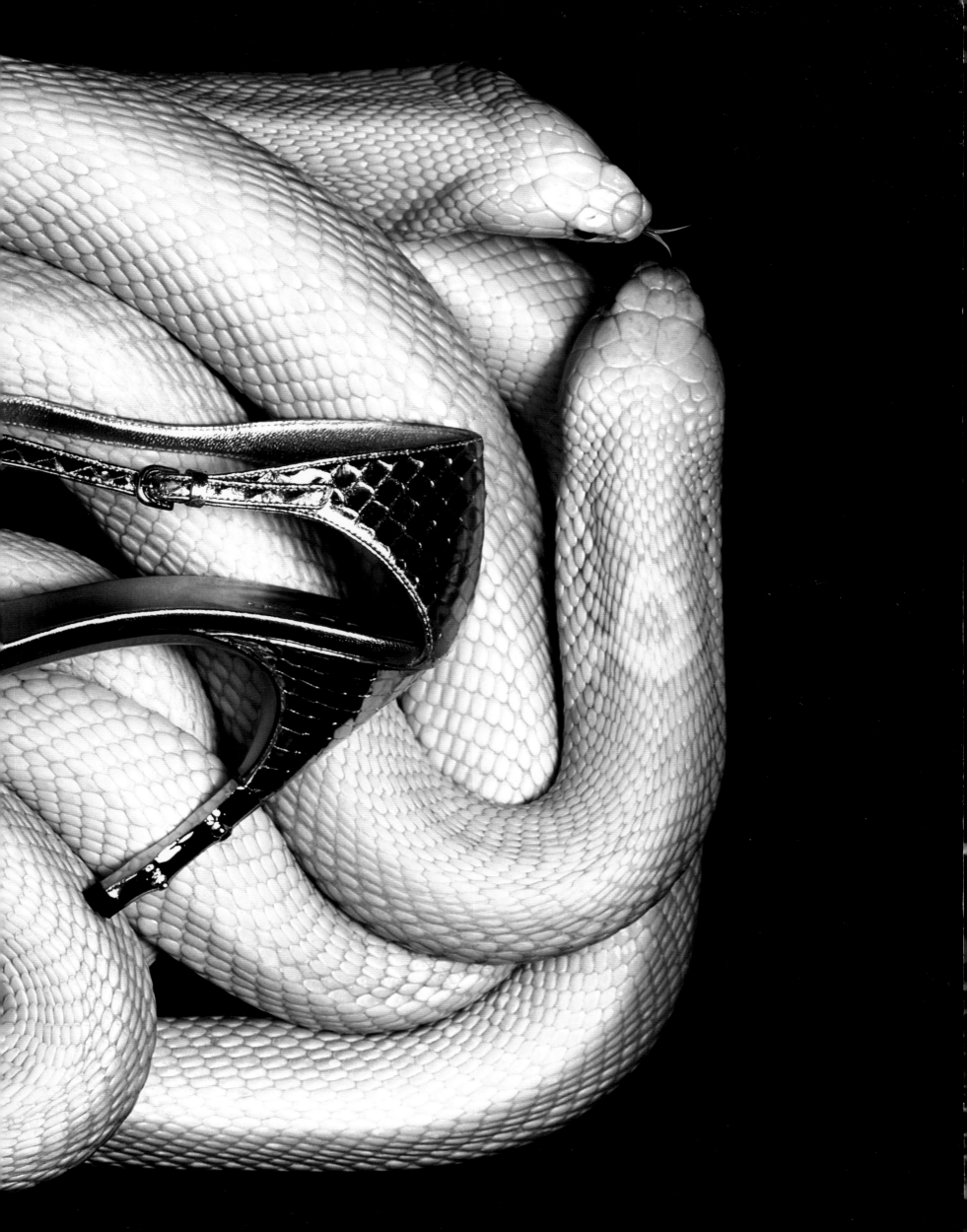

the world of
GUCCI

GUCCI SHOP • NEW YORK

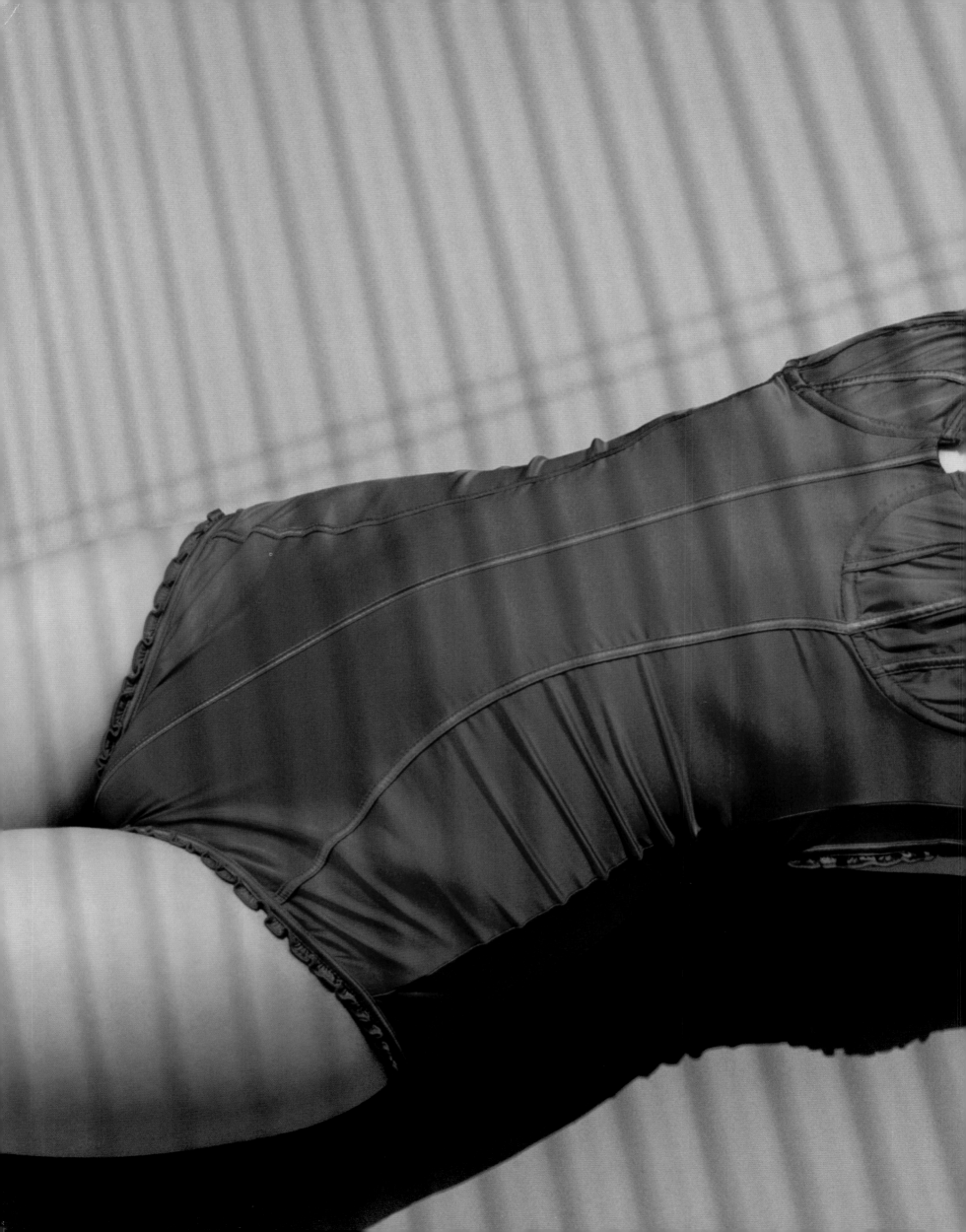

VOGUE

MARC

American
Collections
ew excitements

Paris
Collections
ews digest

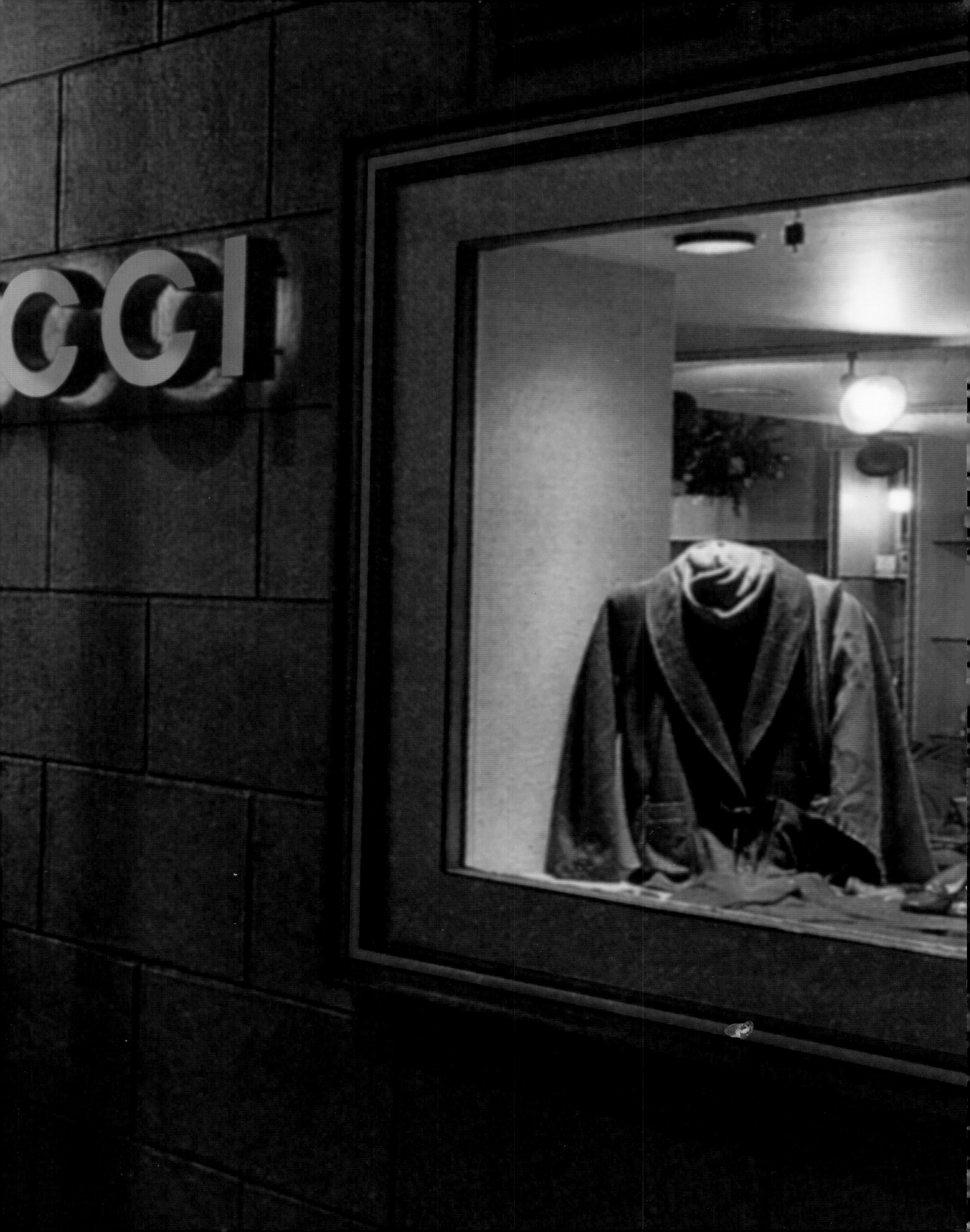

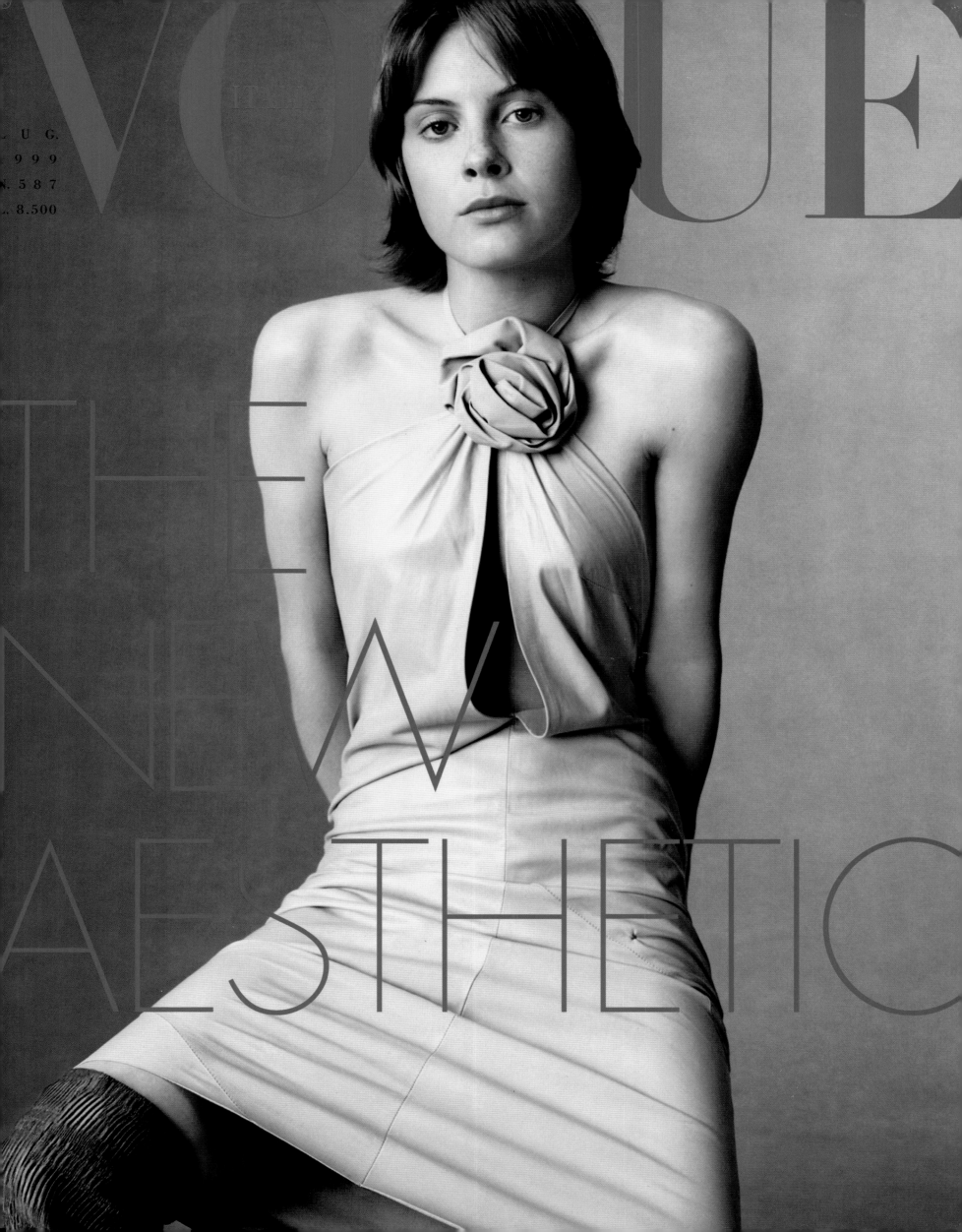

G. GUCCI

(4) FIRENZE FIRENZE **(4)**

Via Vigna Nuova, 7
:: Via Parione, 11 ::
(Angolo Via Vigna Nuova
:: Ponte alla Carraia) ::

G ARTICLES
MAROCCO LEA-
TICLES
RELLES
WALKING STICHS
GS
R ARTICLES

Firenze, il 30-4 1922

Gentilis.mo Sig. B.n G. E. Levi
Città.

Prego sentire se prima non le fu comunicato in_____
_____a quanto stabilimmo di presenza, e m___
mi è ancora possibile dato ch' l'avvocato mio e
_____ per affari. Sarei però a proporle, d_____
lei un punto di questa interiore sulla Gal___
e di poi; le sarò più preciso in merito.
La ringrazio e col massimo _____

Guccio Gucci

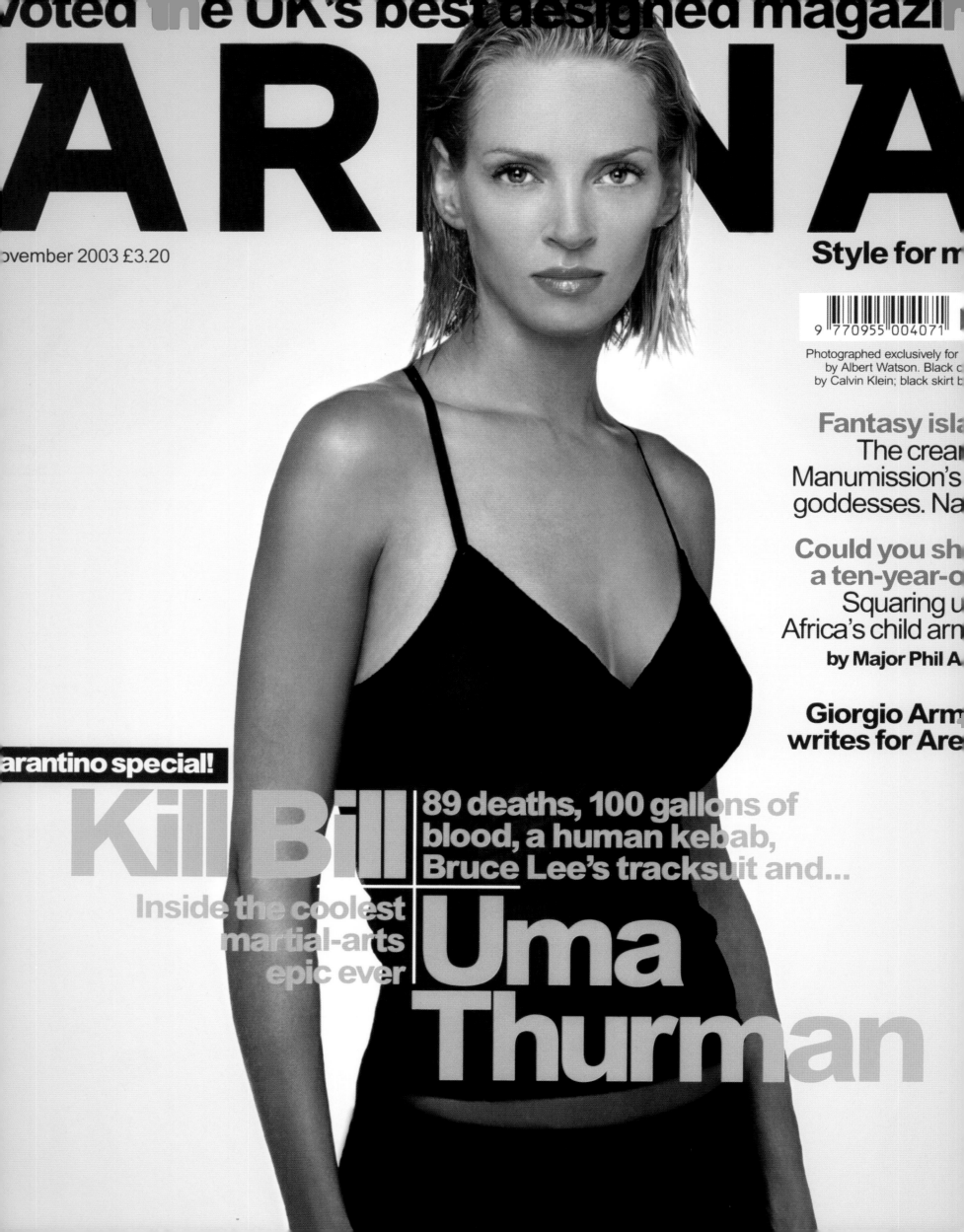

Voted the UK's best-designed magazine

ARENA

November 2003 £3.20

Style for m

Fantasy isla
The crea
Manumission's
goddesses. Na

**Could you sh
a ten-year-o**
Squaring u
Africa's child arn
by Major Phil A

**Giorgio Arm
writes for Are**

arantino special!

Kill Bill

89 deaths, 100 gallons of blood, a human kebab, Bruce Lee's tracksuit and...

Inside the coolest martial-arts epic ever

Uma Thurman

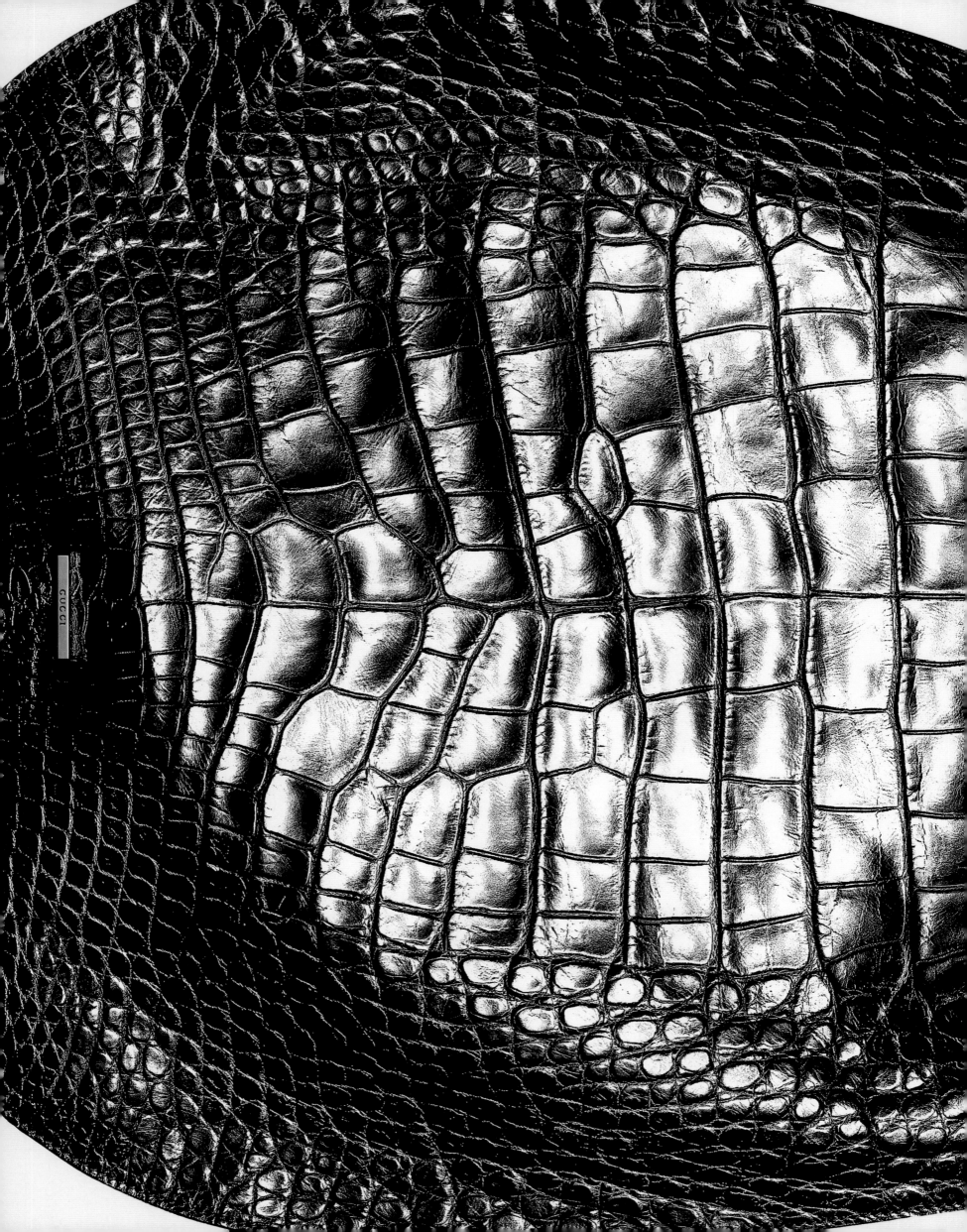

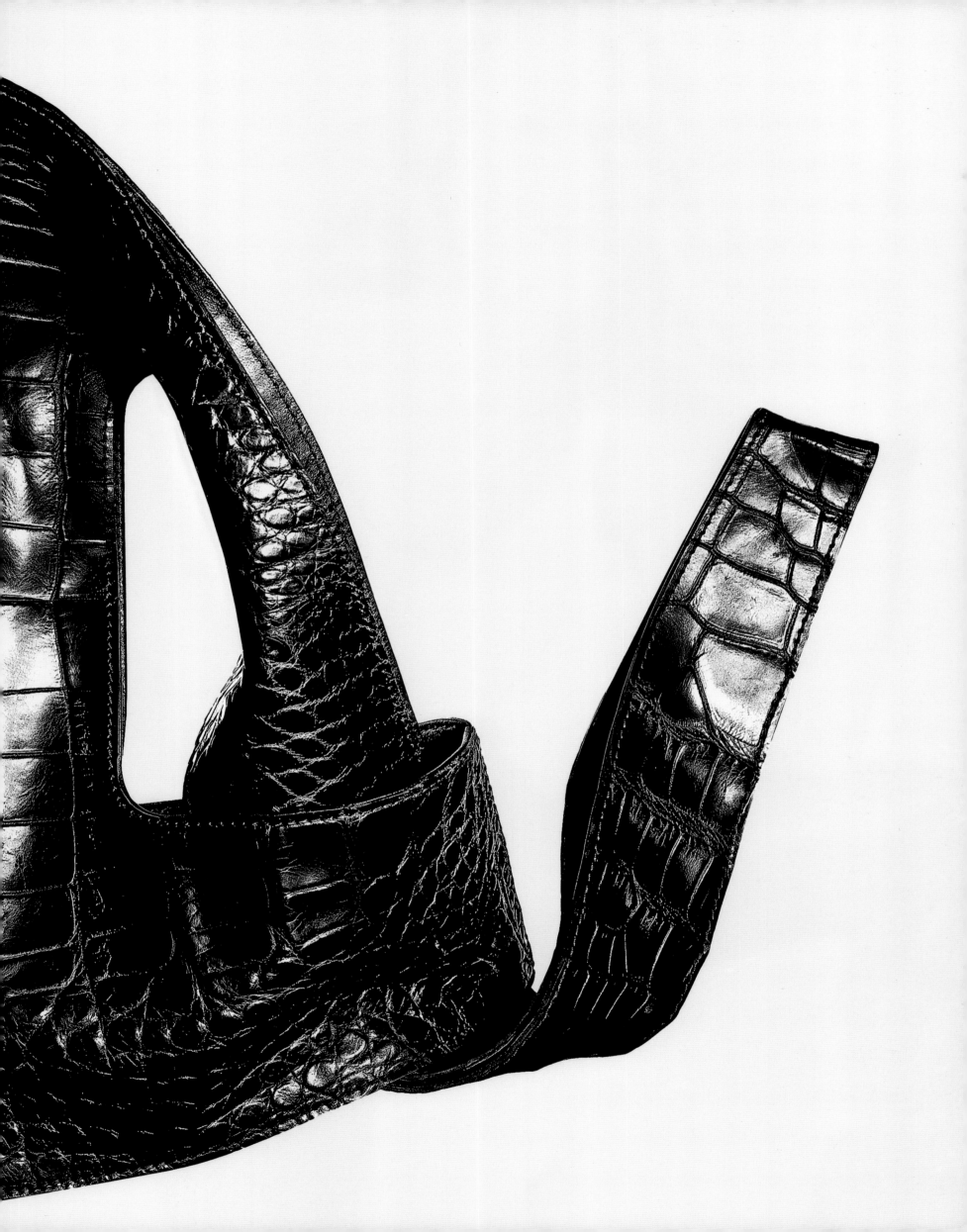

VOGUE

ITALIA

L U G.
2 0 0 1
N. 611
L. 8.500

EXTRAV

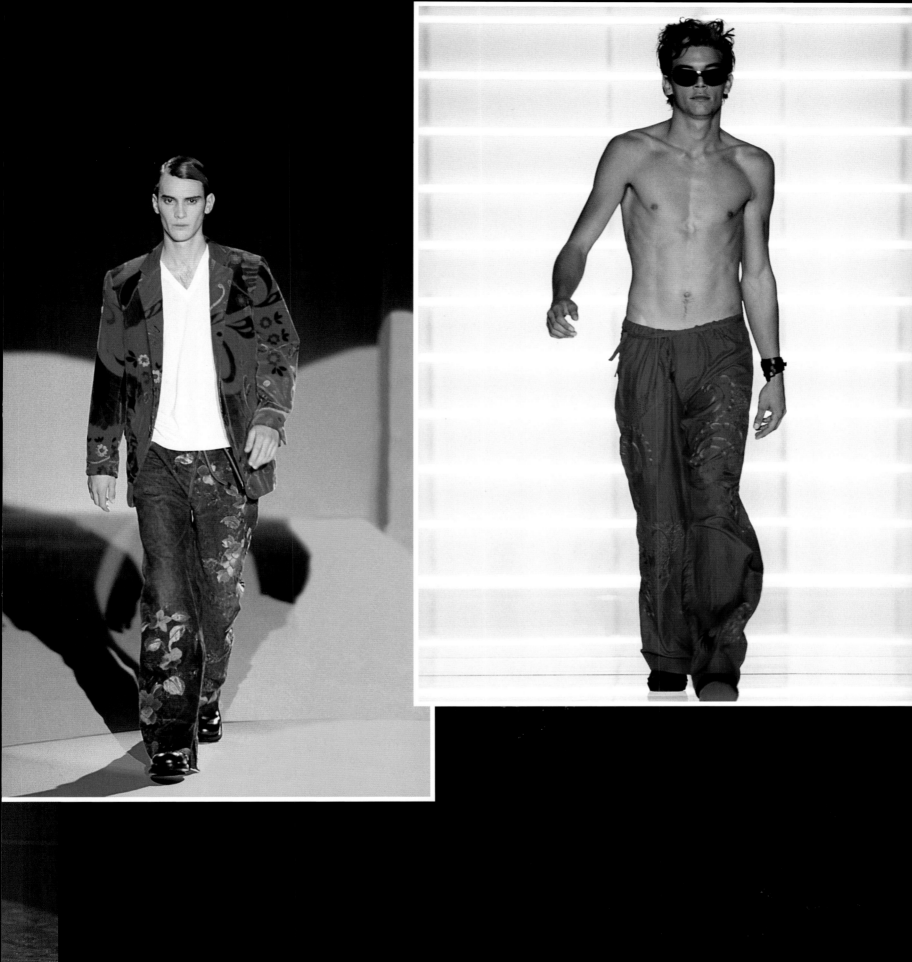

VOGUE
PARIS

vembre N°852

Nicole Kidman
Numéro de charme

Elizabeth Hurley
Les secrets d'un corps

Maradona
Vive l'antihéros

Armani
es muscles
e la réussite

Mode/Sport
50 pages d'interdits

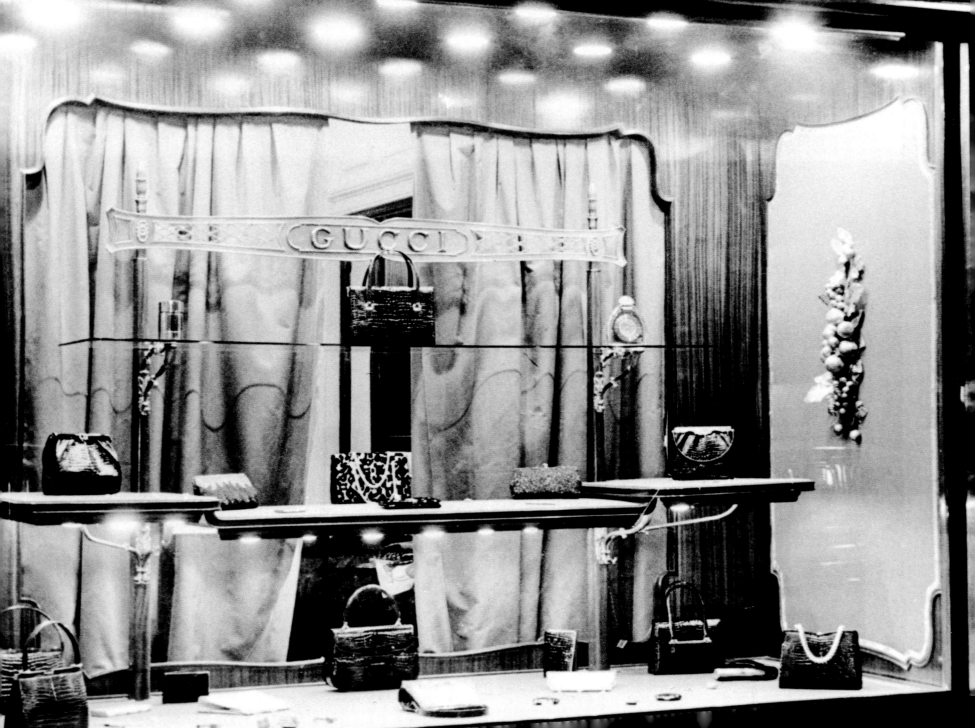

VOGUE

ITALIA

E N.
004
. 641
5,00
aly only

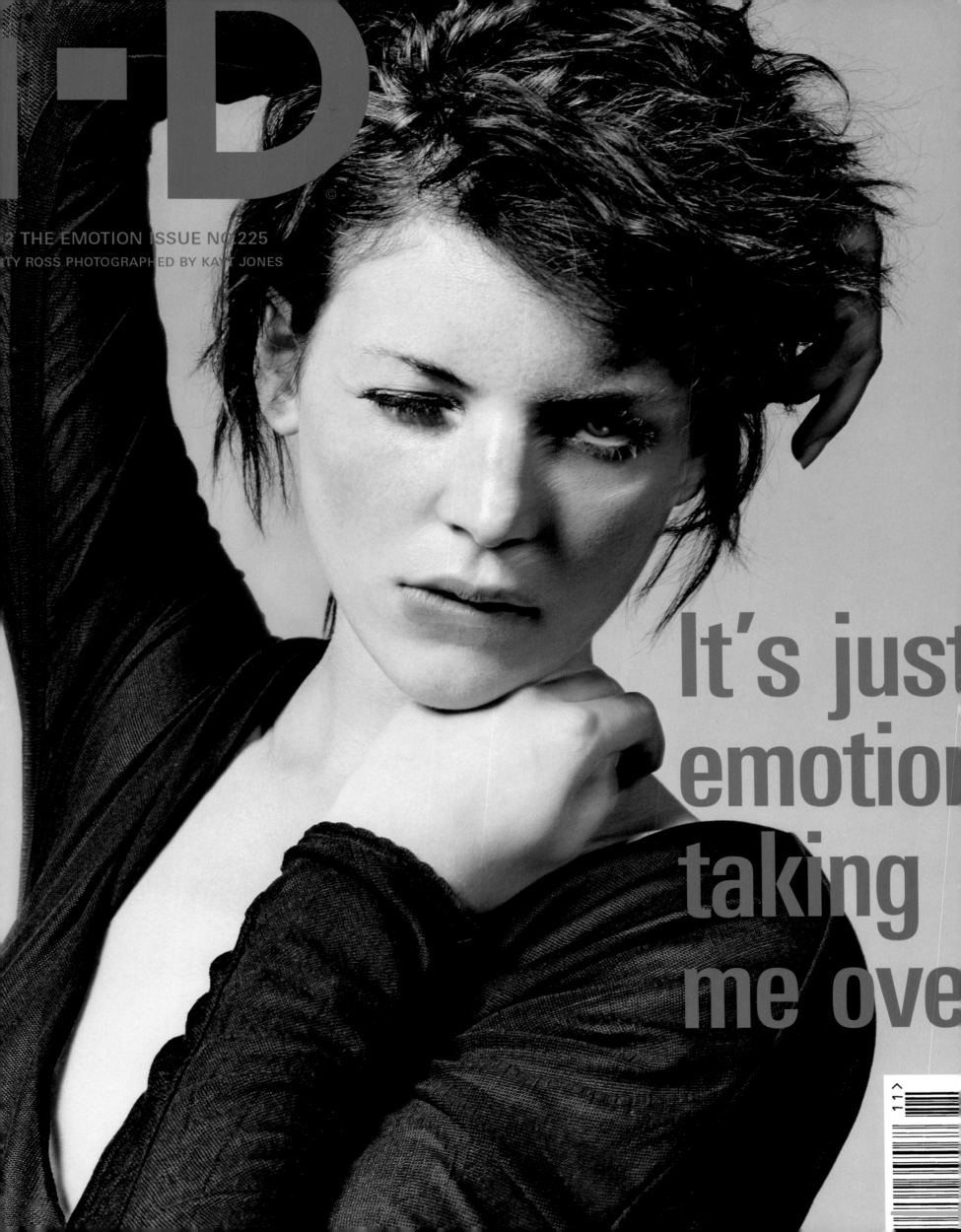

i-D

2 THE EMOTION ISSUE No225

TY ROSS PHOTOGRAPHED BY KAY T JONES

It's just emotio taking me ove

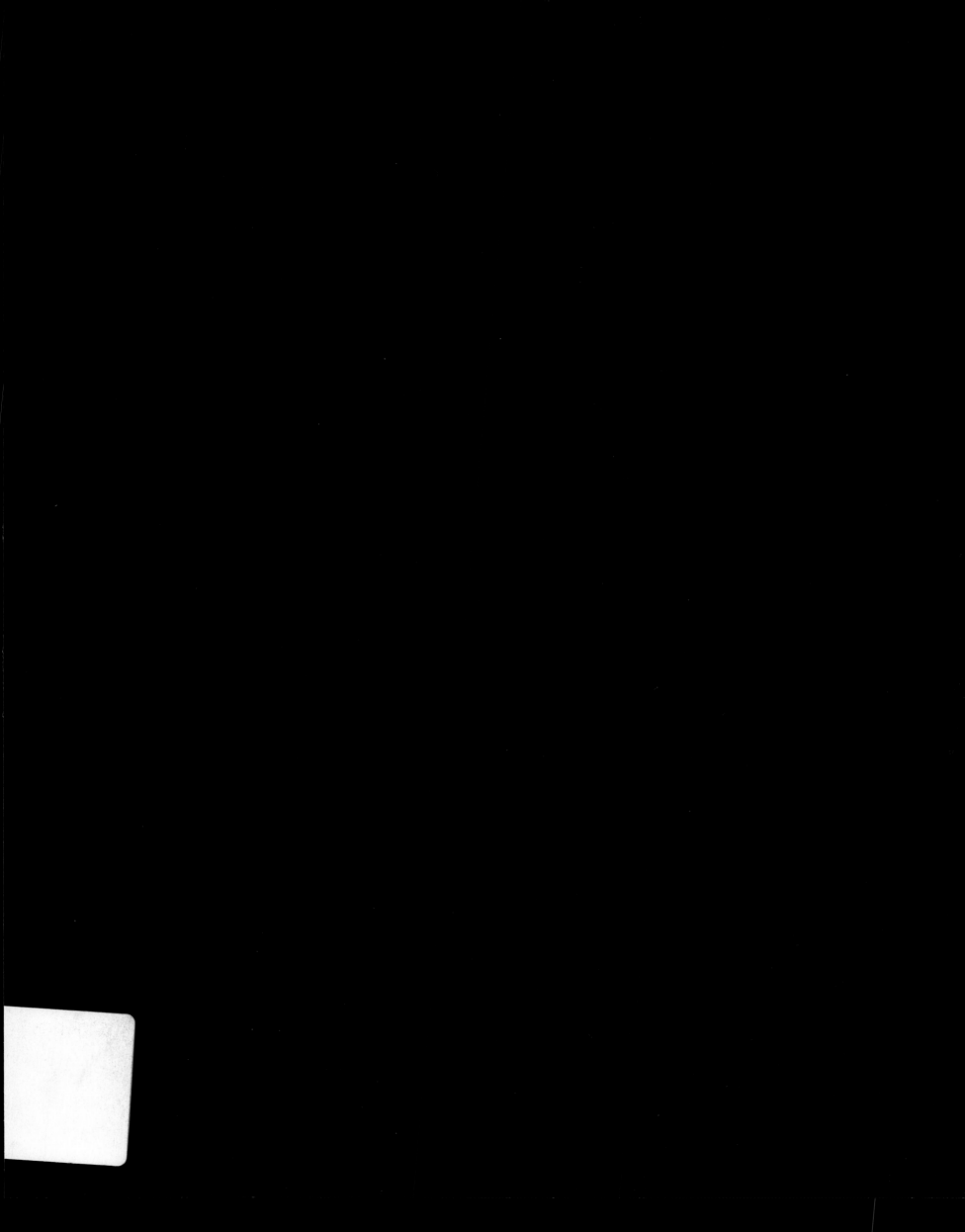

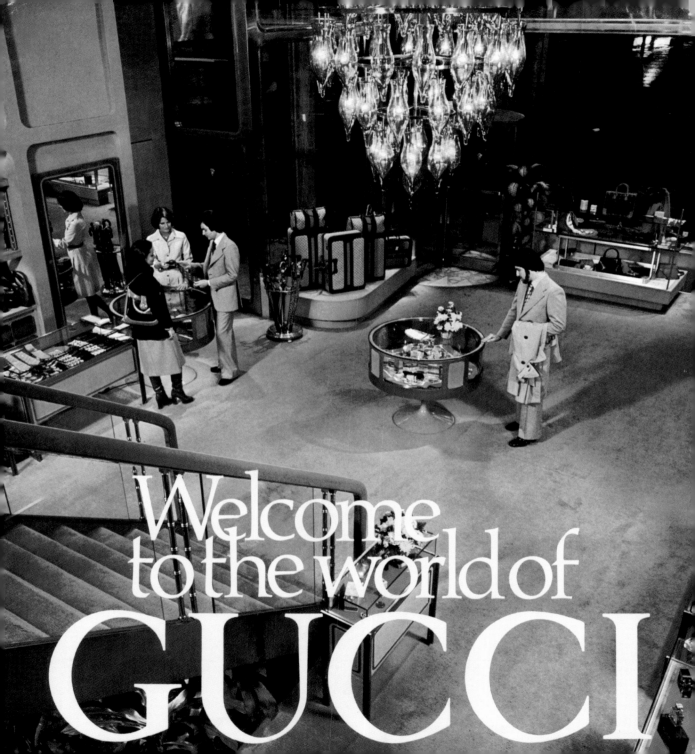

Welcome
to the world of
GUCCI

GUCCI

FIRENZE
73. VIA TOURNABUONI
TEL. 287.251

MILANO
5. VIA MONTENAPOLEONE
TEL. 794.118

ROMA
8. VIA CONDOTTI
TEL. 689.340

ROMA
HILTON HOTEL
TEL. 349.6390

MONTECATINI
15. CORSO ROMA
TEL. 71.094

PARIS
350 RUE ST. HONORE
073-36-13

LONDON
172 NEW BOND STREET
MAYFAIR 2716-7

NEW YORK
699 FIFTH AVE.
(212) 753-0758
(212) 753-9259

BEVERLY HILLS, CALIF.
347 NO. RODEO DR.
(213) 278-3451

PALM BEACH, FLA.
ROYAL POINCIANA PLAZA
(305) 832-6024

VOGUE

PARIS

Mars
N°865

Spécial MODE

*Plein soleil sur
les collections:
tout ce dont
vous allez rêver
& Los Angeles
plein les yeux.*

Exclusif: Sharon Stone,
Bono, *les* Gates,
Jean-Christophe Rufin......
Au nom des autres.

w.vogue.com

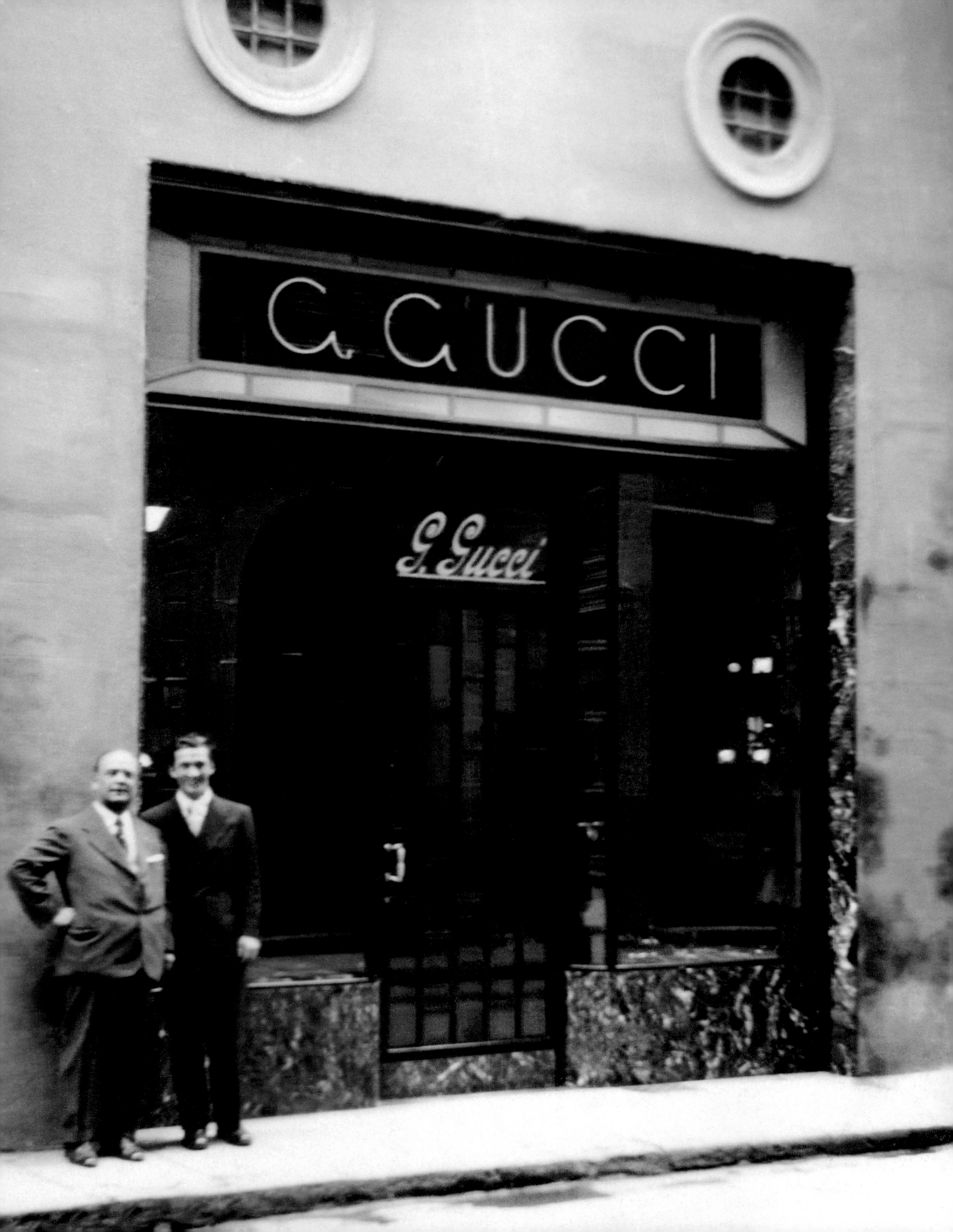
G. GUCCI
G. Gucci

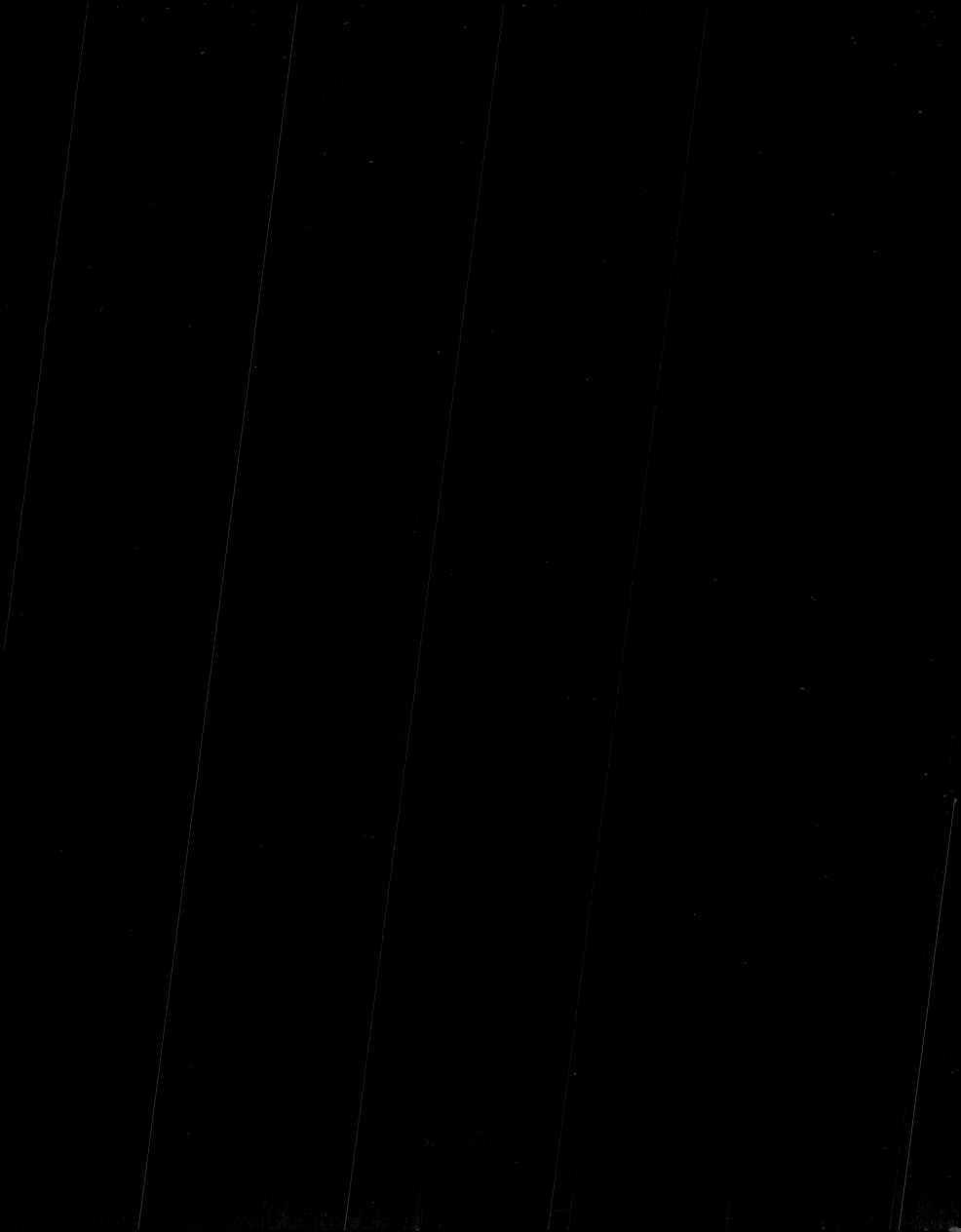

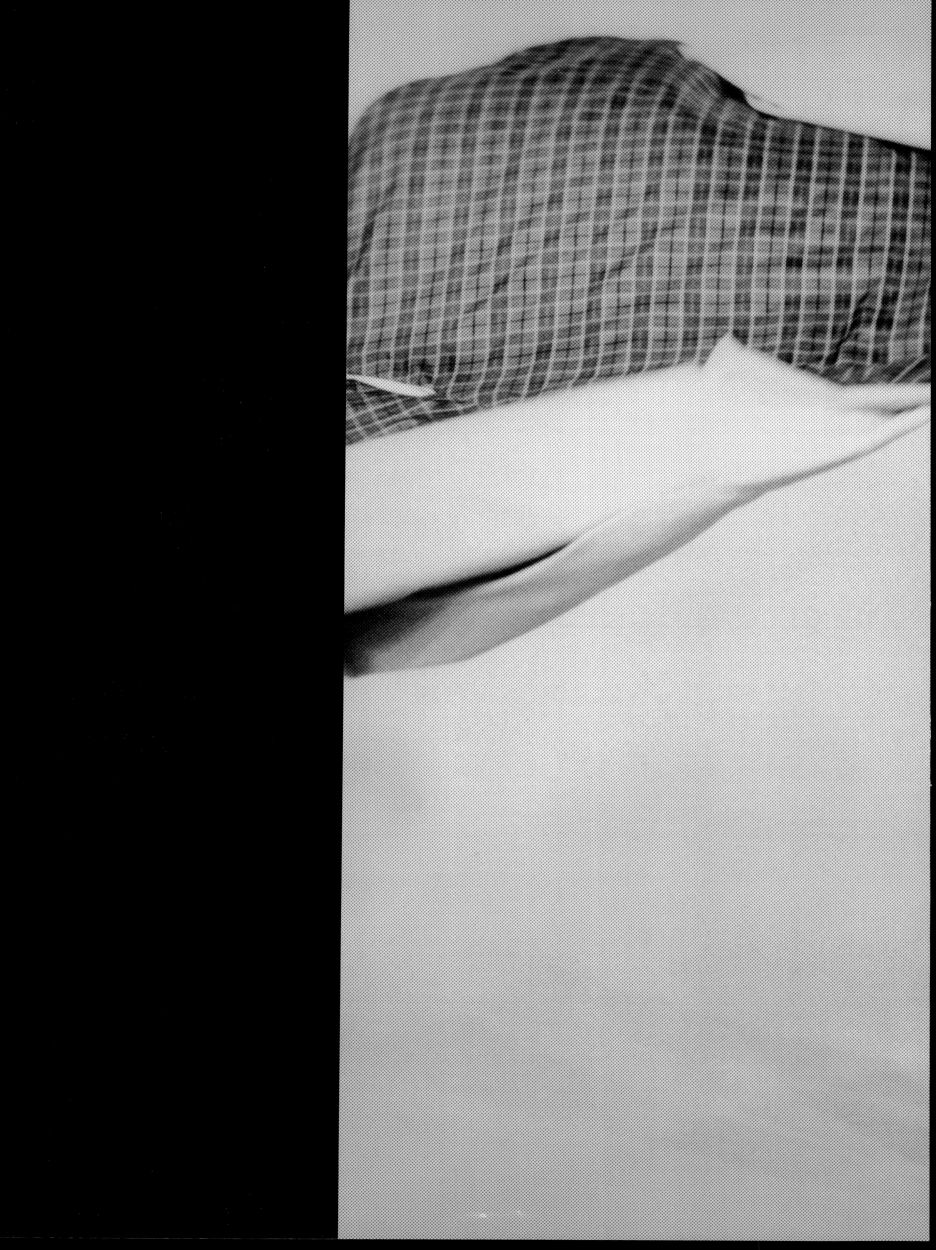

mode passion

Superwomen, le retour / Perfecto absolument / L'allure Anna Mouglalis

Marc Jacobs / Guillaume Canet / Gauguin et la photographie

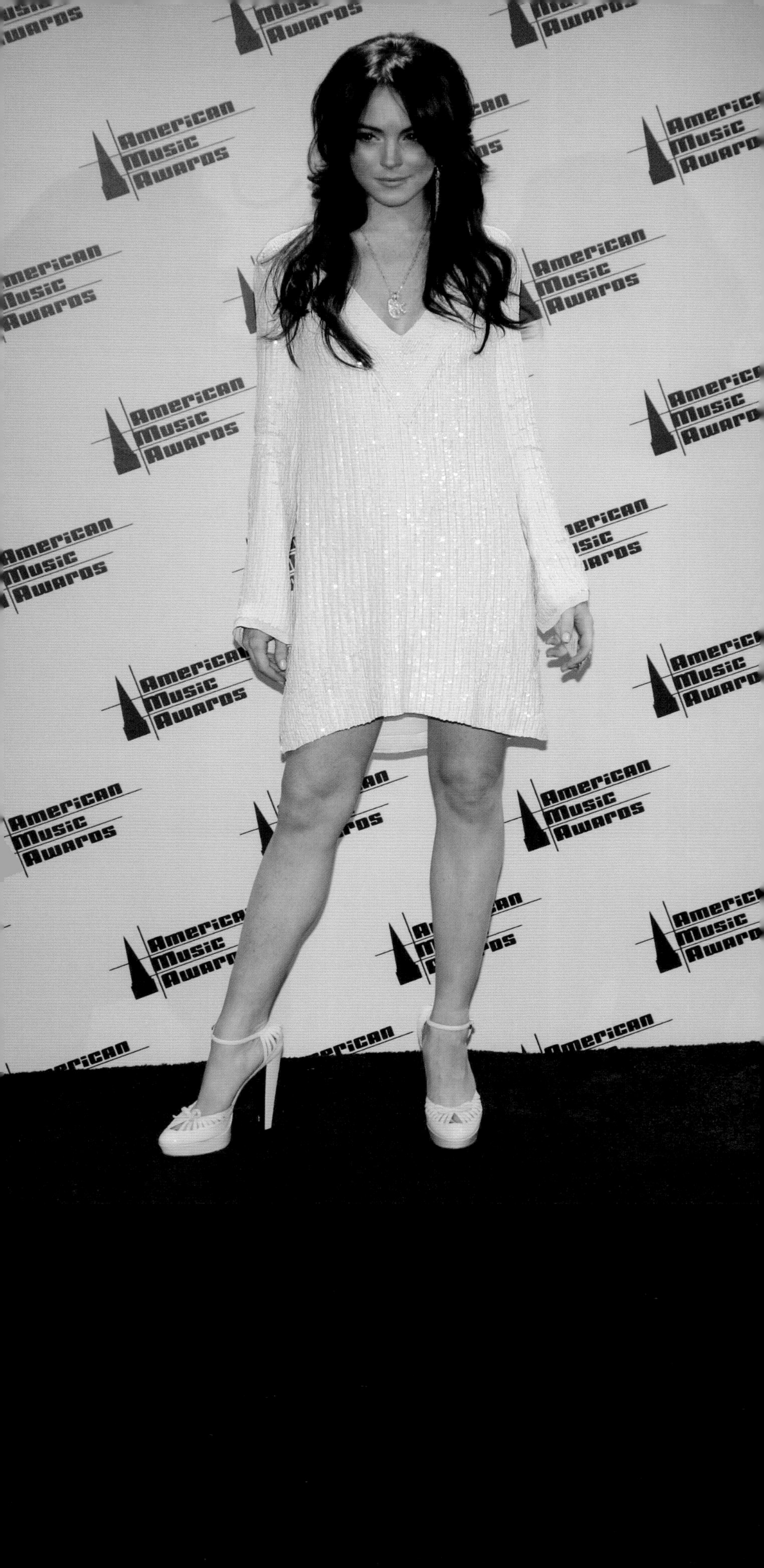
American
Music
Awards

With our

best Compliments.

VOGUE
PARIS

être
ne
femme

élirante
n formes
ofteuse
nceinte
réatrice
résidente
nspirante
ensuelle et
moureuse…

T 5590 - 822 - 30,00 F - 4,57 €

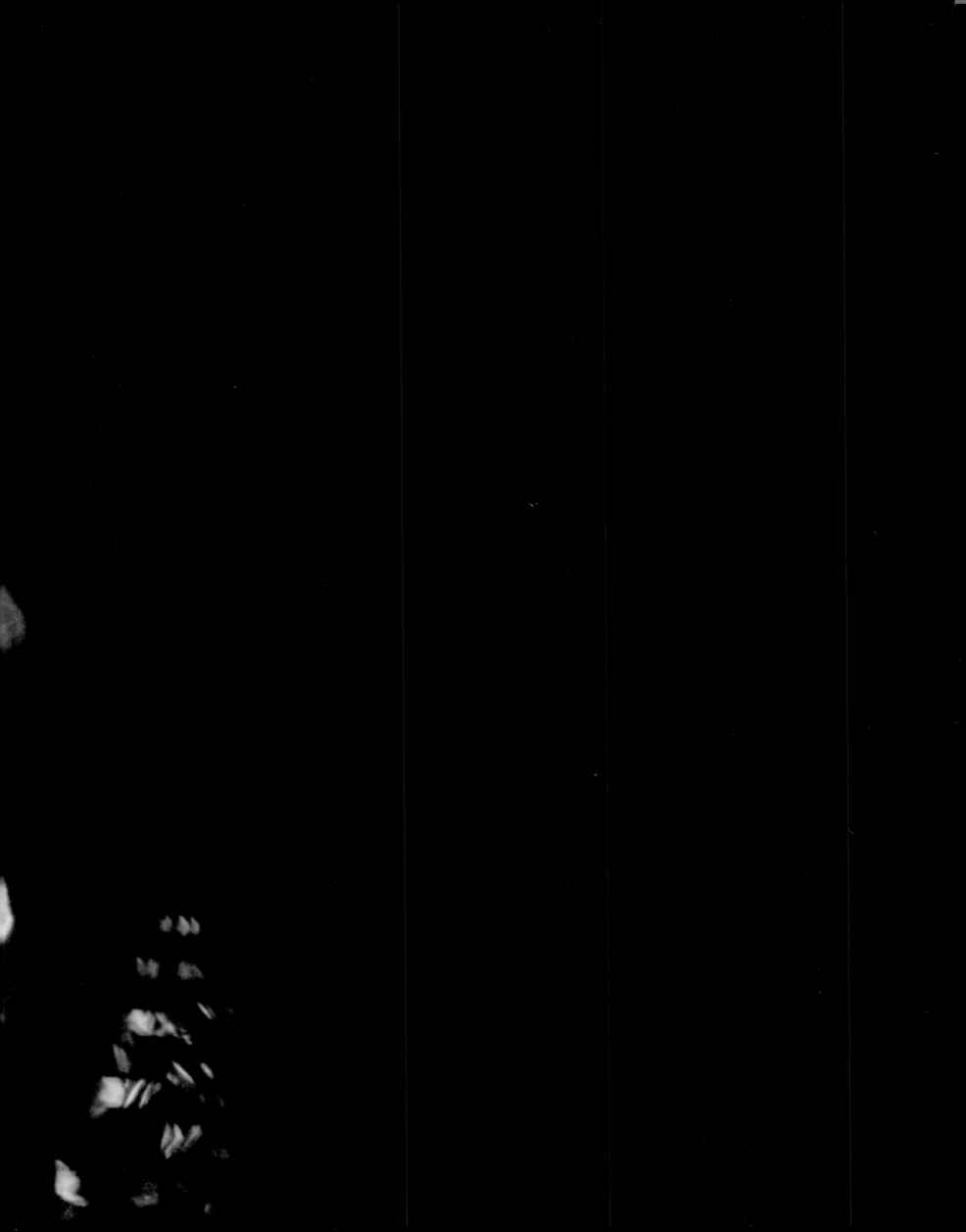

THE BAMBOO
THE HORSEBIT
THE WEB
THE GG
THE GUCCI ICONS

In design terms, it is a pure example of the saying that necessity is the mother of invention – as well as a perfect illustration of the outburst of craftsmanship and design-thinking that put Italy on the map after World War II. The bamboo-handled bag, product-code 0633, was developed in a Gucci backroom in Florence in 1947, by craftsmen who were charged to muster all their powers of innovation to think their way around war-time shortages – yet still make objects that met the Gucci standards of desirable exclusivity. It is not recorded just who looked at a strip of bamboo – which could still be imported from Japan – and thought of turning it into a bag handle; nor who worked out how to cure and bend it into a semi-circle over a Bunsen burner to make it glossily smooth to hold. It was a masterstroke though. Once it was articulated and attached to the bag by four metal loops (using the least amount of the precious commodity possible in the on-site forge), the bamboo handle became a piece of design history belonging to that brilliant streak of Florentine fashion innovation that was simultaneously sending cork-soled wedges and cellophane shoes tripping elegantly out of Ferragamo's workshops.

The allure of the 0633 – with its smartly sportif shape, inspired by a saddle – attracted women from far and wide. It was produced in bright striped canapa canvas for summer holidays and brindled pigskin to match autumn country tweeds and, as shortages began to lift, in increasingly luxurious leathers, ostrich, crocodile, lizard and even sealskin. Over decades, the bamboo went beyond its origins as a pragmatic solution, becoming a device used on generations of new bag shapes, and gradually transforming itself into a Gucci visual code branded into multiplicities of products. Bamboo-inspired patterning has turned up just about everywhere now – from umbrella handles to headscarves, watch-straps and jewellery, and even carved wittily into a pair of golden stiletto heels. It's a part of house heritage – like the horsebit, green-red-green webbing and the GG – that's proved amazingly capable of time-travelling, staking its place in the fashion of the moment according to what the designer feels at the time.

HOW GUCCI HARNESSED THE BRANDING POWER OF AN UNMISTAKABLE PIECE OF HARDWARE...
THE HORSEBIT

As Madonna swept off the stage with her MTV Video Music Award in a flurry of blonde hair in 1995, the silver horsebit belt she was wearing made a simultaneous power-broadcast of its own: "Gucci, Gucci, Gucci!" – words she later laughed on camera. That image – pop-legend revelling in Gucci glamour – electrified fashion-commentators who recognised the clothes from the autumn/winter Seventies-accented Jet-Set collection. The public reaction was instant: store phonelines were jammed by women desperate to get the belt, the shoes, the velvet bootcut hipsters; the everything, in fact. The horsebit – that most Gucci of all Gucci signifiers – glinted, centre-front, in the phenomenon that put the house into vertical take-off. Winking silvery enticement from the toes of block-heeled hologram "carpaint" pumps, it made knowing reference to the traditional Gucci loafer, but jolted it with an unprecedented flash of sexual energy. The jointed brass horsebit was first written into house vocabulary in the Fifties, deployed as a strong punctuation point used on heavy tan leather saddle-stitched handbags. Since then, the double-ring and bar motif has inspired myriad translations. Bits have been both miniaturised and maximised as hardware; luxuriously schemed into embossed or burned-out surfaces on leather suede and velvet; turned into repeat patterns printed on silk and sculpted into the components of precious jewellery. Its decorative potential has twisted from the dainty (the diamond-encrusted bit on the navy duchesse-satin sandals made for Liza Minnelli in the late Eighties) to the fierce – as the expression of post-modern glamour loaded in excess onto the horsebit bags of 2003/04 outrageous patchworks of studded python, crocodile and ostrich, implanted with brazenly overstated brass hardware.

Nowhere, though, has the horsebit played a more crucial role than in marking out the Gucci loafer as a time-traversing design classic. The snaffle, often with a strip of green-red-green slipped under it, was introduced as a decoration on the soft and comfortable brown or black leather Gucci men's moccasins in 1953. In the early years, they graced the feet of Clark Gable, John Wayne and Fred Astaire, and later, when women's versions appeared in 1968, became the choice of sophisticated women looking for a luxurious kind of comfort. Francesco Turchi, Gucci's master-cobbler, perfected the supple design of the loafer in Florence and, as demand rose, began adding refinements. His elaborations for women began by embedding a gold chain in the stacked heel which, added to the horsebit, became another house identifier. By the Seventies, the loafer was a fashion cult in America; an item of such popularity that Gucci opened a store specially dedicated to shoes in New York to service the growing lines of customers. "It comes," declared *The New York Times* in 1977, "bench-made and with a pedigree no other moccasin can ever claim". The range was extended from the classic best-selling $89 men's version, to touch the heights of luxury (crocodile, lizard, ostrich, python), while the women's loafer was also designed for evening in black silk faille and satin, with jewelled heels and bits. The shoes became favourite everyday wear for elegant women such as Lauren Bacall (who has donated several pairs to the collection of the Fashion Institute of Technology). Such was the widespread fame and social resonance of the loafer in America that its meaning was avidly dissected in newspaper columns and what-to-wear business manuals. When the Eighties saw the new classes of Yuppies and executive women climbing the career ladder, they were shod in Gucci loafers. As Lisa Birnbach's book *Going to Work* reported from Los Angeles in 1980 what "powerful feet are wearing" was "the Gucci men's loafer, $195 per pair, and the Gucci women's loafer two-inch pump, $225 per pair." Its casually clubbable, confident style enshrined the Gucci loafer both as a corporate American status symbol and as an unchanging fashion-proof design classic. Its basic template, though, has also proved simultaneously capable of being played up and tuned to the beat of changing fashion. By the Nineties, the women's horsebit loafer was lifted way out of its original conventional conservative context and wittily and ironically revamped as clogs, spa shoes and sexily sharp-toed stilettos. Meanwhile, the men's Gucci loafer, reborn in advertising campaigns, became – in a flash – a fashion fetish object, a seducer's shoe, the sign of a confident hedonist luxuriating in every temptation.

In new times, Frida Giannini looks at the horsebit with fresh eyes. She might take the prints of interlocking, squared-off bits, of the highly fashionable red and blue Gucci pattern used for shoulder bags, shoes and silk blouses in 1969-1970, transform them in her computer, and project them, in mini-form, onto flowing dresses or blown up to exaggerated scale on travel-totes. With new style, a new feminine touch, that counts as the current instalment in the long-running serial of Gucci design.

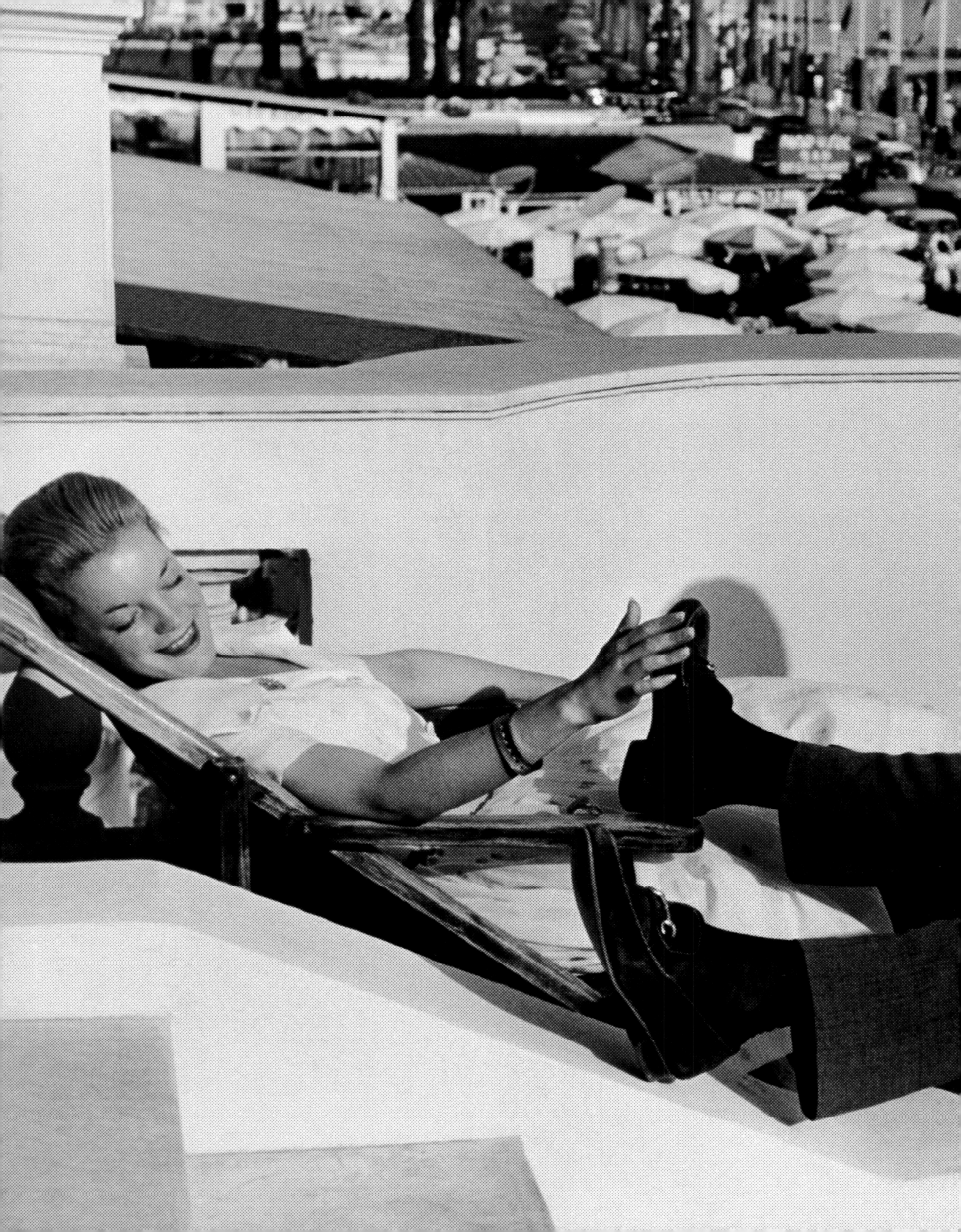

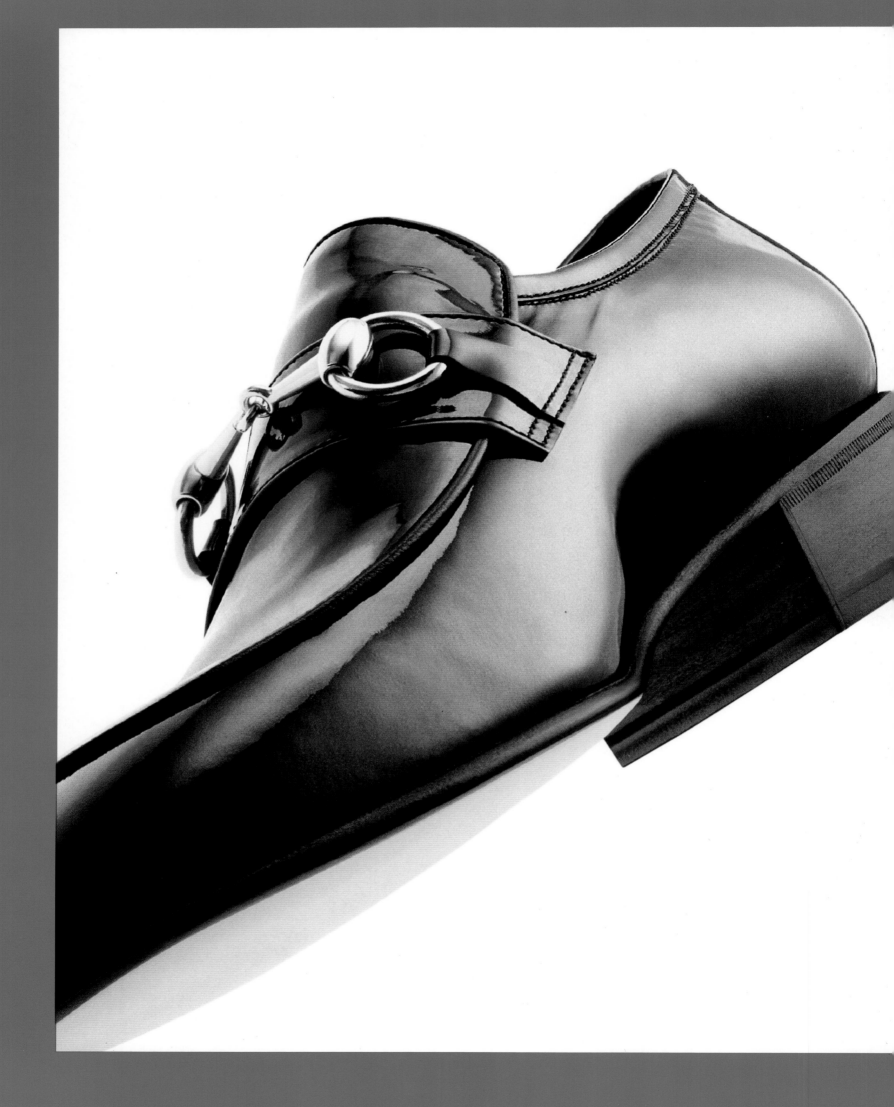

TWO COLOURS, THREE STRIPES:
THE GREEN-RED-GREEN CODE
THAT MARKED OUT GUCCI AS A
DESIGN THOROUGHBRED...

THE WEB

The idea – simple and strong and amazingly enduring – came out of the stable. Based on a girth-strap – the strip of canvas webbing used to secure a saddle to the back of a horse – it was co-opted by Guccio Gucci as a neat allusion to the sporting interests of the moneyed equestrian classes, which – so went the suggestion – his Florentine forefathers had been around for centuries. The last part wasn't quite true, but no matter: the webbing is the material of the at-a-glance flash of communication that has signalled Gucci-ness across continents and cultures, and way into the next century. Its genius – the green-red-green colour combination – was settled upon as an unswerving house standard sometime in the early Fifties – is an historical masterstroke of "branding", decades before that term was ever dreamed up.

A six-inch vertical strip of the green-red-green ribbon was implanted, centre-front, in the prototype "Jackie O" bag of 1961 – a design trick that had been applied to distinguish Gucci suitcases since the Fifties. It has been used as straps for shoulder bags ever since the Sixties; for signature belts and trimmings on clothes – from tan Seventies A-line skirts to 21st century bikinis. It's been spliced into Gucci loafers forever. In 1979, the Gucci stripes liveried the interior of possibly the flashiest sedan the Seventies ever produced: a Gucci-designed limited-edition Cadillac Seville. The green-red-green running along dashboard, door-linings and across headrests, was smoothly described in the brochure as "immediately identifying you as a connoisseur of Gucci". By then, of course, the green-red-green had raced way beyond its origins to become a shorthand visual signifier of Gucci's visual identity. Horsiness practically forgotten, by the Eighties it was deployed on almost any product – on keyrings, flasks, table-lamps, magazine racks, picnic cases and playing cards. In the Eighties, it turned up as trimming for sportswear, turning Gucci's tennis shoes into an early example of designer trainers, a concept knowingly revisited in 2004. Now, its ability to flex across time, fashion and mood is being turned in fresh directions – always surprising, but then again, always the same.

PARIS
BEVERLY HILL
PALM BEACH
CHICAGO
HONG-KONG

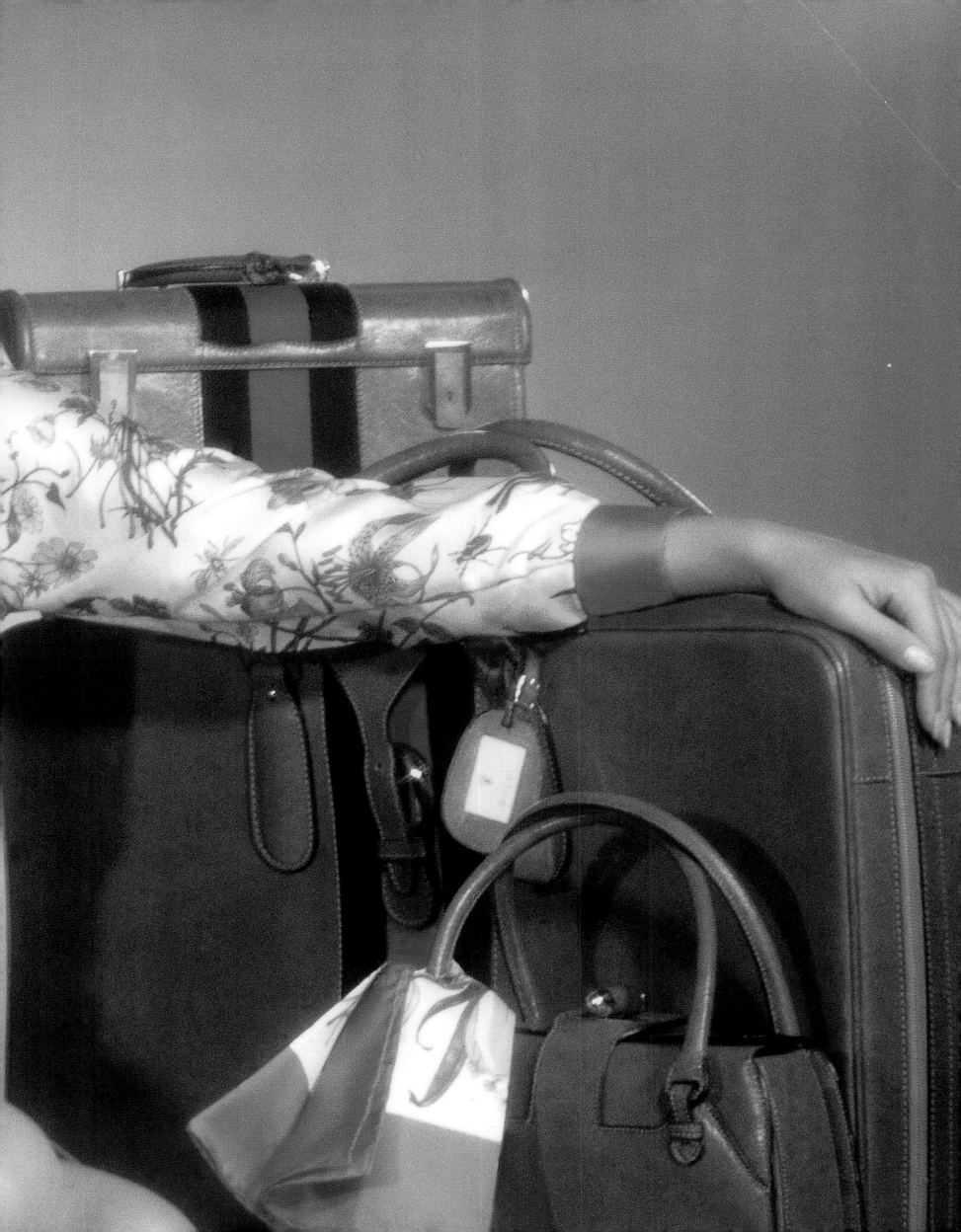

THE GG

When Amber Valletta stepped in front of Mario Testino's camera for the Gucci autumn/winter 1995/96 advertising campaign, the belt-buckle she was wearing on her midnight-blue velour hipster pants was as good as a worldwide announcement: the GG was back. That big circle of interlocking silver metal Gs was an obvious flashback to the jet-set heyday of Gucci and a kind of flash-forward, too, marking the beginning of a renewed rush of success. As accurately as that big chrome GG buckle evoked the cool, smooth, curved international hipster look of Seventies design, it was not a literal reproduction of any of the dozens of examples of GG hardware stored in the archives. That though, also put it directly in line with the way the initials of the company's founder have been visually engineered to meet the moment since the beginning.

Guccio Gucci's initials were first used in the early Sixties – as either single or double Gs – as squared-off fastenings for bags which were developed and made in Gucci's own forge at the Via delle Caldaie in Florence. Transferred soon after into a diamond-shaped pattern woven into the best-selling cotton canvas luggage, the GG monogram transported the company's fame, quite literally, around the globe in the much-photographed company of movie-stars, aristocrats and celebrities. The "GG Canvas", a brown diamond pattern on an ecru ground initially reserved for suitcases, sports bags and shoulder bags, frequently came trimmed with the green-red-green ribbon for extra stylistic punch (a rarer variant appeared in blues with a blue-red-blue stripe). From the mid-decade, keeping pace with the Space-Age interest in all things modern, the company experimented with plasticising the canvas with a layer of resin to make it waterproof, later improving the quality by applying multi-layers of poly-vinyl durable enough to withstand the rigours any airport baggage handlers could throw at it.

The multiple uses of the GG increased exponentially thereafter. In 1968, to coincide with the opening of the Beverly Hills store, a leap of transference installed the GG into the introductory line-up of Gucci's first ever ready-to-wear clothing, an idea pushed through by Paolo Gucci from design in Italy. This small but unmissable addition to Gucci's repertoire included leather-trimmed mini-kaftans, with matching low-heeled Go-Go boots and, later, suits, coats and men's raincoats. Prime early examples of the blatantly confident top-to-toe branded "total look", the idea bounced back, with an extra spin of irony, in a capsule GG canvas clothing and accessory collection of 2000, timed perfectly to hit the "logomania" craze. Reconfigured and deployed in innumerable designs and redesigns, the eternal GG has appeared and reappeared over time, merged into a circle, back-to-back, inverted, abstracted. It's been done in silver and gold, burned into luxurious velvet embossed into leather, stamped onto suede, printed on silks, woven into jacquards, patchworked together in luxurious crocodile and lizard. A status symbol that crosses cultures, it has acquired an elasticity of popular meaning that stretches its possibilities to include high glamour and, when the moment arises, a knowing sense of humour.

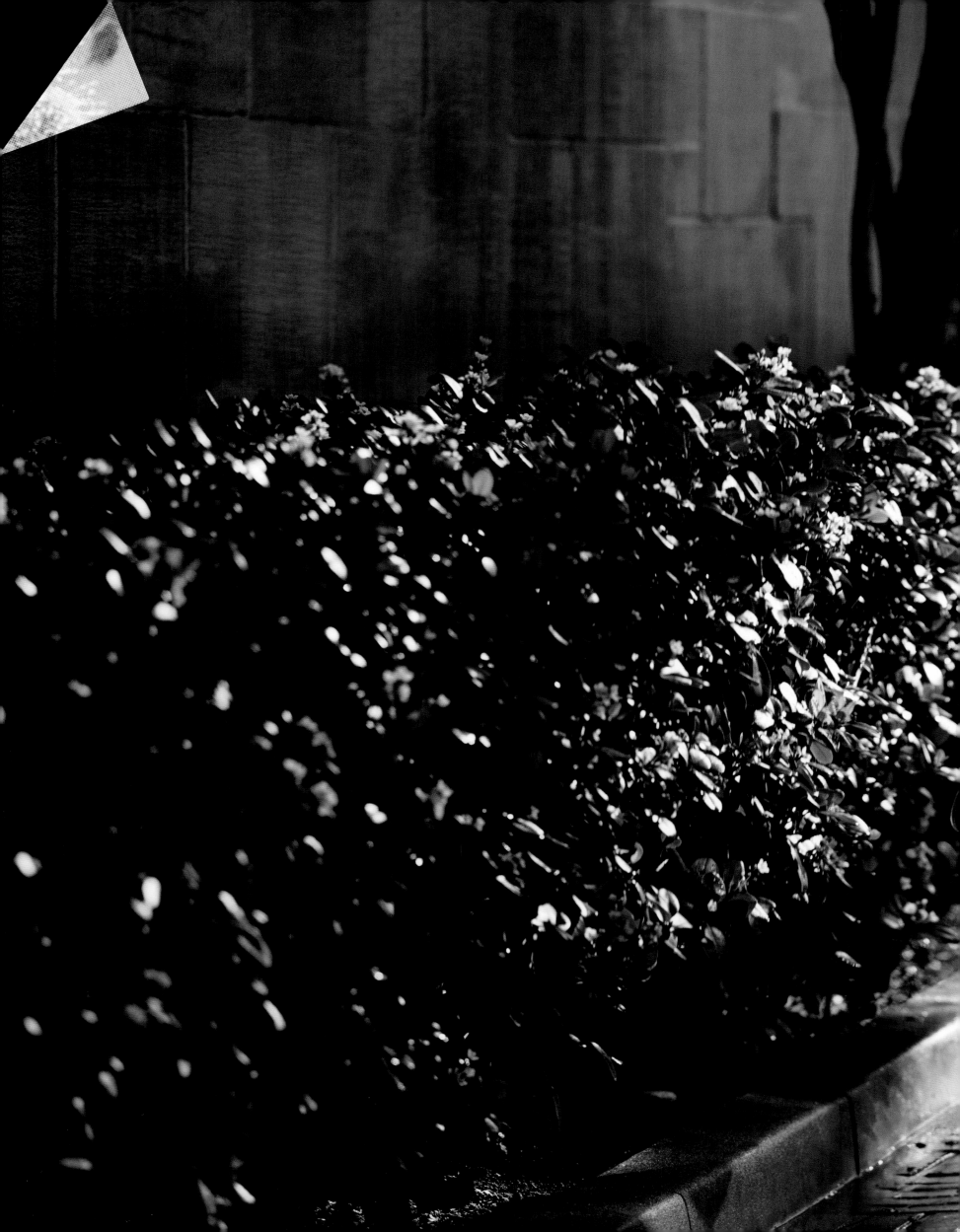

GUCCI BY GUCCI

85 years of Gucci

1881
Guccio Gucci is born in Florence

1897
He finds work in the Savoy Hotel, London

1902
He returns to Florence and joins the leather manufacturer Franzi

1905
Aldo Gucci is born to Guccio and his wife Aida

1907
Vasco Gucci is born

1912
Rodolfo Gucci is born

1921
Guccio opens the Gucci business in Florence with
stores at Via Vigna Nuova, and then Via del Parione

1960

The New York store is moved to a prestigious Fifth Avenue address, next to the St Regis Hotel

1951

Rodolfo opens first Milan store at Via Montenapoleone

Around this time, the green-red-green web becomes a hallmark of the company

1938

The Rome store opens on Via Condotti

1935-36

As a result of the League of Nations embargo against Italy, Gucci finds alternatives to imported leather and other materials. It develops a specially woven canapa or hemp from Naples, printed with the first signature print – a series of small interconnecting diamonds in dark brown on a tan background, of which Gucci's first successful suitcases are made

1953

Gucci becomes one of the pioneers of Italian design in the US when Aldo opens the first American store in the Savoy Plaza Hotel, East 58th St, New York

Guccio Gucci dies at the age of 72

The Gucci loafer with metal horsebit is created

1955

The Gucci crest is registered as trademark

1947-48

Production of leather goods resumes after World War II. Aldo Gucci introduces the pigskin that becomes a signature house material

The first bamboo-handled bag, inspired by the shape of a saddle, is thought to be produced in this period

Maurizio Gucci is born to Rodolfo and his wife Alessandra

1961

The bag subsequently known as "Jackie O" is launched; around this time the GG logo is applied to canvas and used for bags, small leather goods, luggage and the first pieces of clothing

Gucci stores open in London and Palm Beach

1966

The "Flora" scarf print is designed for Princess Grace of Monaco

1972

Gucci opens in Tokyo

Maurizio Gucci, son of Rodolfo, goes to work with his uncle Aldo in New York, until 1982

Around this time, Gucci is hitting the heights of fashionability. A new store dedicated to clothing is opened at 699 Fifth Avenue in New York, while 689 Fifth Avenue is opened to specialise in shoes, bags, luggage and accessories

1974

Gucci opens in Hong Kong

1975

The first Gucci perfume is launched

1982

Gucci becomes an S.p.A. and leadership eventually passes to Rodolfo Gucci

1963

The first Paris store opens

1968

Gucci opens in Beverly Hills

1981

The Gucci ready-to-wear collection parades for the first time at the Florentine fashion shows at the Sala Bianca, playing heavily on the Flora print

1985

The Gucci loafer is displayed at the Metropolitan Museum of Art in New York and becomes part of the permanent collection

1996

Tom Ford's autumn/winter 1995/96 collection of "Jet Set" glamour is a massive hit, putting Gucci back at the forefront of fashion

1990

The American designer Tom Ford is hired to over-see women's ready-to-wear

1994

Tom Ford is appointed Creative Director

1989

The Anglo-Arab holding company Investcorp purchases 50 per cent of Gucci shares

1993

Maurizio Gucci transfers his shares to Investcorp, ending the family's involvement in the firm

1995

Domenico De Sole, previously Chief Executive Officer of Gucci America Inc, is appointed Gucci Group's Chief Executive Officer

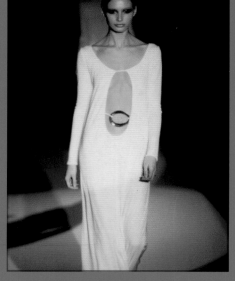

1996–97

Tom Ford's collection of white cutout jersey dresses fastened with abstract horsebit belts sets the sleek, sexy, modern style of the Gucci Nineties look and establishes it as a house dedicated to the kind of evening glamour that attracts swathes of Hollywood actors and actresses

1999–2001

Gucci's name becomes associated with Gucci Group when the strategic investment of PPR (Pinault Printemps Redoute at the time) begins focusing on building a portfolio of luxury brands of which Gucci is still the largest

2004

Tom Ford and Domenico De Sole leave the company

1999

The "Jackie O" bag is relaunched in many colours and variations, triggering a huge and sustained response. It opens the era of the Gucci must-have "It" bag

2002

Frida Giannini, previously a bag designer for Fendi, joins Gucci's accessory department, contributing bold reinventions of house signatures as part of Ford's team

2005

Frida Giannini, from the previous role of Creative Director of Accessories, is appointed Creative Director of Women's ready-to-wear after her relaunch of the Flora print as a bag collection proves a huge success

2006
Frida Giannini is also appointed Creative Director
for Menswear

2006

Gucci Rome store, Via Condotti
8, 1960s

Princess Grace of Monaco,
Gucci Rome store, Via Condotti
21, 1950s

Sophia Loren, Gucci Rome store,
1970s

Princess Caroline of Monaco,
1973

Sammy Davis Junior and his wife,
London Airport, 1981

Aldo Gucci, Gucci New York
store, Fifth Avenue, 1972

Princess Soraya of Iran, Gucci   Jodie Foster, Gucci Rome store,
Rome store, 1970s   1970s

Rod Stewart, London Airport,   Roman Polanski, Paris, 1975
1976

Peter Sellers and Miranda
Quarry, London Airport, 1970

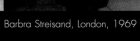

Roger Moore in *The Man with*   Barbra Streisand, London, 1969
the Golden Gun by Guy
Hamilton, 1974

Jacqueline Kennedy Onassis and   Lawrence Harvey, Gucci Rome
John F. Kennedy Junior, Palm   store, 1960s
Beach Airport, 1973

Clark Gable and Aldo Gucci,   Ursula Andress, Gucci Rome
Gucci Rome store, 1950s   store, 1960s

Elizabeth Taylor and Richard Burton, Rome, 1962

Anita Ekberg, Rome, 1960s

Britt Ekland in *The Man with the Golden Gun* by Guy Hamilton, 1974

Philippe Niarchos, Paris, 1972   Jacqueline Kennedy Onassis, New York, 1970

Ursula Andress and Jean Paul Belmondo, Rome, 1966

Audrey Hepburn, Rome, 1960s

Princess Grace and Prince Rainier of Monaco, Paris, 1956   Tony Curtis and his wife, Gucci Rome store, 1970s

Claudia Cardinale, Gucci Rome store, 1960s   Elke Sommer, Gucci Rome store, 1970s

Audrey Hepburn, Rome, 1964

Michael Caine and his wife Shakira, London Airport, 1977

Princess Grace of Monaco, Paris, 1966   David Niven and his wife, London Airport, 1971

Olivia Hussey, Gucci Rome store, 1960s   Joan Collins, Gucci Rome store, 1960s

Liza Minnelli and Joel Grey, 1972

Ad Campaign S/S 2006, Iselin Steiro and Freja Beha, Photo Craig McDean

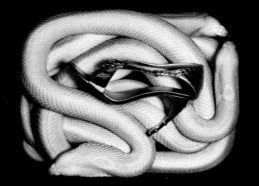

Vogue Paris, March 2004, Kate Moss, Photo David Sims

Ad Campaign S/S 2004, Photo Guido Mocafico

GQ Germany, April 2002, Brad Pitt, Photo Herb Ritts

Vogue USA, July 2002, Caroline Murphy, Photo Craig McDean

Madonna, London, November 2005

Vogue Italia, July 2000, Hannelore Knuts, Photo Steven Meisel

Ad Campaign F/W 2002-03, Natalia Vodianova, Photo Mario Testino

Ad Campaign F/W 2002-03, Eduardo Braun, Photo Mario Testino

Backstage S/S 2006, Elena Bagucci

Gucci catalogue, 1978, Gucci New York store

Gucci Madrid store, 1980s

Backstage S/S 2006

Vanity Fair USA, February 2004, Gwyneth Paltrow, Photo Michael Thompson

Vanessa Redgrave, *Blow Up* by Michelangelo Antonioni, 1965 — Backstage

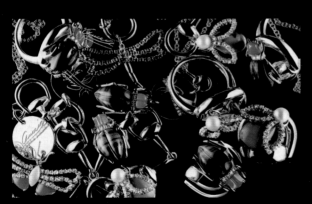

Ad Campaign Jewelry, S/S 2006, Photo Guido Mocafico

Fashion shows: F/W 2000-01, S/S 2003, S/S 2003, S/S 2004, F/W 2006-07

W Magazine, March 2005, Kate Moss, Photo Mert Alas & Marcus Piggot

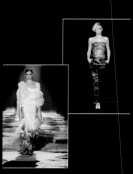

W Magazine, March 2003,
Elise Crombez, Photo Mert Alas
& Marcus Piggot

Fashion shows: F/W 2004-05,
S/S 2001, F/W 2006-07,
S/S 2003

Vogue Italia, December 2000,
Zoe Gaze, Arles, France, 2000,
Photo Peter Lindbergh

Numéro, May 2003, Karen
Elson, Photo Sølve Sundsbø

Charlize Theron, Academy
Awards, Los Angeles, February
2004

Vogue USA, March 1957,
Joanne Friedman, Photo Clifford
Coffin

Ad Campaign S/S 1998, Photo
Guido Mocafico

Vogue Paris, March 2005,
Daria Werbowy, Photo Mikael
Jansson

Ad Campaign F/W 2004-05,
Photo Guido Mocafico

Beyoncé Knowles, New York,
October 2003

Vogue Italia, July 1999, Juliet
Elliott, Photo Steven Meisel

Ad Campaign F/W 1995-96,
Amber Valletta, Keith Mallos and
Andrea Boccaletti, Photo Mario
Testino

Ad Campaign F/W 2001-02,
Steven JR Gallison, Photo Terry
Richardson

Francis Ford Coppola, San
Francisco, 1970

Madonna, MTV Studios, New
York, October 2005

Vogue Italia, January 2003, Elise
Crombez, Photo Steven Meisel

Guccio Gucci's letter, Florence, 1924

Veruschka, Rome, 1971

Craftsmen, Gucci Florence workshop, late 1940s

Linda Carter, London Airport, 1980s

Ad Campaign S/S 1999; Robert Konjic, Photo Mario Testino

Arena, November 2003, Uma Thurman, Photo Albert Watson

George Clooney, Academy Awards, Los Angeles, March 2006

Gucci London store, Sloane Street, 1998

Jodie Foster, 1977

Fashion shows: F/W 1996-97, F/W 1999-00, S/S 2006, F/W 1999-00

Gucci Photo Shooting, 1970s

Ellen Barkin, Los Angeles, 1998

Cameron Diaz, 2005

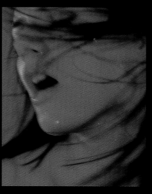

W Magazine, November 1999, Jennifer Aniston, Photo Michael Thompson

Numéro, September 2003, Tiiu Kuik, Photo Greg Kadel

Ad Campaign "Gucci Rush", 1999, Malgosia Bela, Photo Mario Testino

Vogue Italia, July 2001, Karolina Kurkova, Photo Steven Meisel

Pharrell Williams, Grammy Awards, Los Angeles, February 2006

Fashion shows: F/W 1999-00,
S/S 1992, F/W 1998-99,
F/W 1995-96

Gucci Cadillac Seville, 1979

Gucci catalogue, S/S 1989,
Photo John Goodman

Ad Campaign S/S 2004, Photo
Mario Testino

Photo John Rawlings, 1955

Numéro Homme, February
2005, Fu'ad, Photo Greg Kadel

Gucci Family, Florence, 1982,
Giorgio, Maurizio, Roberto,
Aldo, Alessandro, Paolo,
Elisabetta, Patrizia, Guccio, and
Rodolfo in front of the stairs

Gucci Beverly Hills store, 1980s

Pop Magazine, March 2005,
Karen Elson, Photo Mert Alas &
Marcus Piggot

Jim Kimberly and his wife, Lake
Worth, Florida, April 1968

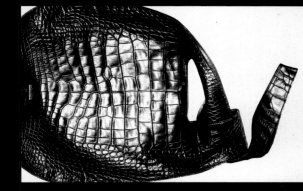

Vogue Paris, April 2000, Frankie
Rayder, Photo Herb Ritts

Ad Campaign F/W 2001-02,
Photo Guido Mocafico

Fashion shows: F/W 2003-04,
S/S 2005, F/W 1999-00,
S/S 2001

Ad Campaign F/W 2001-02,
Erin Wasson and Steven JR
Gallison, Photo Terry Richardson

Gucci New York store, 1980s

Details, March 2005,
Guilherme Schell, Photo Mikael
Jansson

Ad Campaign F/W 2004-05,
Daria Werbowy, Photo Mario
Testino

Vogue Paris, November 2004,
Kate Moss, Photo Mario Testino

Charlize Theron, Beverly Hills,
Los Angeles, November 2005

Gucci catalogue, 1971

Gucci Florence store, 1960s

Fashion show S/S 2004, Photo
Biasion Studio/WireImage

Gucci Photo Shooting, early
1970s - Backstage

Gucci Milan store, 1980s

Vogue Italia, January 2004,
Gemma Ward, Photo Steven
Meisel

Gucci Florence store, 1980

Numéro, May 2004, Natasha
Poly, Photo Vincent Peters

Pop Magazine, Spring/Summer
2005, Photo Toby McFarlan
Pond

Ad Campaign "La Pelle
Guccissima", F/W 2005-06,
Photo Craig McDean

Gucci Florence workshop, Via
delle Caldaie 7, 1953

Gucci catalogue, F/W 1985-86, Photo Fabrizio Ferri

Numéro, October 2005, Photo Vincent Peters

Fashion show S/S 2004, Julia Steigner

Peter Ustinov, Rome Gucci store, 1964

Ad Campaign, F/W 1998-99, Photo Guido Mocafico

L'Uomo Vogue, May 1998, Photo Steven Meisel

Samuel Beckett, S. Margherita Ligure, Genoa, 1971

Claudia Cardinale, *La ragazza di Bube* by Luigi Comencini, 1963 – Backstage

Vogue USA, February 2003, Natalia Vodianova, Photo Craig McDean

Ad Campaign S/S 1980, Photo Alberta Tiburzi

Vogue UK, February 2001, Sarah Jessica Parker, Photo Regan Cameron

Ad Campaign F/W 1998-99, Chris Walters, Photo Steven Klein

W Magazine, July 2003, Daria Werbowy, Photo Mario Sorrenti

Vogue Italia, July 1996, Kylie Bax, Photo Steven Meisel

Naomi Watts, Venice Film Festival, September 2003

Numéro, October 2001, Linda Evangelista, Photo Mert Alas & Marcus Piggot

Peter Sellers, London, 1969

Vanity Fair Italia, September 2004, Elizabeth Hurley, Photo Ruven Afanador

W Magazine, October 2002, Gisele Bundchen, Photo Fabien Baron

Gucci catalogue, F/W 1985-86, Photo Fabrizio Ferri

Ad Campaign F/W 2004-05, Maximiliano Patanè and Daria Werbowy, Photo Mario Testino

Ad Campaign S/S 1995, Chandra North and Shiraz Tal, Photo Mario Testino

Vogue Italia, January 2004, Missy Rayder, Photo Steven Meisel

Arena Homme Plus, October 2005, Andres Segura, Photo Inez van Lamsweerde & Vinoodh Matadin

Gucci Florence store, Via Vigna Nuova 47, 1956

Vogue Australia, July 2000, Photo Tony Notarberardino

Ad Campaign F/W 2001-02, Photo Terry Richardson

Linda Christian, Gucci Rome store, mid 1960s

Fashion show F/W 1996-97, Trish Goff

Vogue USA, October 1961, Wendy Vanderbilt, Photo Horst P. Horst

Liv Ullmann and Edward Albert in 40 Carats by Milton Katselas, 1973

Sarah Jessica Parker, Tony Awards, New York, June 2003

Vogue Paris, December 2002, Gisele Bundchen, Photo Mario Testino

Fashion shows: S/S 1999, F/W 2000-01, F/W 1995-96, F/W 2006-07, S/S 2003, S/S 2002

The Prince of Wales, Windsor, 1983

Gucci catalogue, 1975, Gucci New York store

Ad campaign S/S 1991, Photo
Lance Stadler

W Magazine, Special Jewelry,
April 2004, Karen Elson, Photo
David Sims

Ad Campaign S/S 2003,
Carmen Kass and Ivan De
Pineda, Photo Mario Testino

Fashion shows: S/S 2003,
F/W 2006-07, S/S 2006,
S/S 2002, S/S 2005

Jamie Foxx and Kanye West,
Grammy Awards, Los Angeles,
February 2006

i-D, November 2002, Liberty
Ross, Photo Kayt Jones

Craftsmen, Gucci Florence
workshop, 1953

Gucci advertising, Harper's
Bazaar USA, October 1967

Fashion show F/W 1992-93,
Helena Christensen

Backstage F/W 2006-07, Freja
Beha

Richard Prior and Bill Cosby in
California Suite by Herbert Ross,
1978

Harper's Bazaar USA, April
1955, Photo Louise Dahl-Wolfe

Vogue UK, February 2003,
Photo Tom Munro

Ad Campaign Timepieces, F/W
1998-99, Photo Steven Klein

Numéro, February 2002, Luca
Gaudjus, Photo Thomas Schenk

Vogue USA, July 1956, Photo
Horst P. Horst

Sophia Loren in La Moglie del
Prete by Dino Risi, 1971

Johannes Von Thurn Und Taxis, Acapulco, January 1978

Britt Ekland, Gucci Rome store, early 1970s

W Magazine, August 2000, Jennifer Lopez, Photo Michael Thompson

Marcello Mastroianni and Maria Schell in *Le Notti Bianche* by Luchino Visconti, 1957

Ad Campaign 85th Anniversary, F/W 2006-07, Caroline Trentini and Iselin Steiro, Photo Craig McDean

Pop Magazine, March 2006, Karen Elson, Photo Glen Luchford

Gucci Photo Shooting, New York, early 1970s

Ad Campaign F/W 1996-97, Georgina Grenville, Photo Mario Testino

Ad Campaign F/W 1996-97, Georgina Grenville, Photo Mario Testino

Joanne Woodward and Paul Newman, 1960s

Fashion shows: F/W 1996-97, S/S 1993, F/W 2006-07, S/S 1999

Matt Dillon in *Drugstore Cowboy* by Gus Van Sant, 1989

Veruschka, Rome, 1971

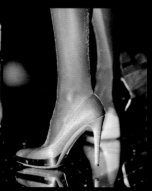

Fashion show F/W 2006-07

Fashion show S/S 2003, Natalia Vodianova

Vogue USA, October 1959, Photo Henry Clarke

i-D, September 2005, Jessica Stam, Photo Satoshi Saikusa

Gucci catalogue, 1968

Sarah Jessica Parker and Mikhail Baryshnikov in *Sex and the City*, Paris, January 2004

Ad Campaign S/S 1998, Photo Guido Mocafico

W Magazine, April 2005, Gemma Ward, Photo Paolo Roversi

Gucci catalogue, 1971

W Magazine, August 2002, Kate Moss, Photo Michael Thompson

Vogue Paris, March 2006, Sharon Stone, Photo David Sims

Benicio Del Toro, Cannes Film Festival, May 2005

Vogue Italia, March 2004, Jennifer Connelly, Photo Nathaniel Goldberg

Aldo Gucci, Gucci Rome store, Via Condotti 21, 1950s

W Magazine, April 2005, Natalia Vodianova, Photo Michael Thompson

Vogue Italia, October 2002, Mila Jovovich, Photo Paolo Roversi

Craftswomen, Gucci Florence workshop, 1953

Ad Campaign S/S 2001, Kate Moss, Photo Inez van Lamsweerde & Vinoodh Matadin

Numéro Homme, September 2005, Marilyn Manson, Photo Ali Mahdavi & Suzanne von Aichinger

Ad Campaign *"Gucci Envy"* Fragrance, F/W 1998-99, Frankie Rayder and Emil Kullanger, Photo Mert Alas & Marcus Piggot

Guccio and Rodolfo Gucci, Gucci Florence store, Via Vigna Nuova 47, late 1940s

Ad Campaign S/S 1999, Photo Mario Testino

Gucci still life, mid 1960s

Fashion shows: F/W 1997-98,
F/W 2001-02, F/W 2005-
06, F/W 2005-06, F/W
1998-99

Yul Brynner, Los Angeles, 1956

Britt Ekland, Milan Airport,
1965

Ad Campaign Timepieces,
F/W 2002-03, Photo Sølve
Sundsbø

Vogue Paris, December 2005,
Gemma Ward, Photo Mario
Sorrenti

Ad Campaign F/W 1997-98,
Photo Mario Testino

Gucci Photo Shooting, mid
1970s

Gucci catalogue, F/W 1987-
88, Photo Fabrizio Ferri

Harper's Bazaar Japan, January
2006, Ai Tominaga, Photo
Leslie Kee

Peter Sellers, Gucci Rome store,
1970s

Fashion shows: S/S 1997,
F/W 2003-04, F/W 1998-
99, F/W 2001-02, F/W
2006-07

Gwyneth Paltrow, MTV Music
Awards, New York, September
1996

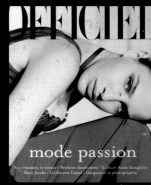

L'Officiel de la Couture et de la
Mode de Paris, September
2003, Mor Katzir, Photo Michel
Mallard

Vogue Paris, May 2005, Raquel
Zimmermann, Photo David Sims

Gucci Rome store, Via Condotti
8, 1980s

Ad Campaign S/S 1996,
Photo Mario Testino

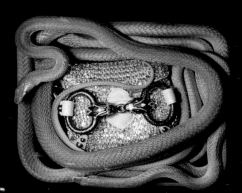

Ad Campaign S/S 2004, Photo
Guido Mocafico